WHAT PEOPLE ARE SAYING
ABOUT *RESTORED*

"Betrayal is the ultimate breach to a relationship that was once filled with love and respect. Tracy Glass exposes the enemy's desire to use betrayal to derail and cause lasting harm. Tracy is not a pretender. She is a courageous and humble woman who never dreamed she would face betrayal in her marriage. I love this book and highly recommend it to anyone who has suffered betrayal. Of course, it addresses separation and divorce, but betrayal can also happen in any relationship.

Scriptures are woven into each chapter, helping, and encouraging the reader to connect God's truth to the author's journey of restoration. Tracy's vulnerability will bless your own journey of healing. You will know you are not alone. There is no wound outside of God's power to heal and bring restoration. Healing awaits you in this book."

—Brenda Zamorano
Biblical Prayer Counseling, Hope in Life Ministry

"Honest. Healing. Hope-filled. Heroic.

When I picked up Tracy's new book, *Restored*, I felt like I was sitting down with a wise, caring friend. This book is an honest, healing, and hopeful guide for anyone navigating the pain of a broken marriage. Tracy's compassionate insights and practical advice provide a heroic sense of reassurance and direction. It's not just a book. It's a heartfelt companion on the journey to healing and renewal. I truly believe this transformative read will touch and uplift anyone who opens its pages."

—Dawn Damon
Author of *The Making of a BraveHearted Woman*

"Walking through a divorce was a traumatizing season of my life some years ago. A divorce can leave you emotionally shipwrecked. I found myself scratching my head wondering if God had forsaken me during that devasting and tumultuous storm. He promises to never leave us or forsake us, and, in that promise, He proved himself to be God to me personally. I learned to lean hard on Him and not my own understanding. Isaiah 54:6 states 'You were like an abandoned wife, devasted with grief, and God welcomed you back.'

I experienced a deeper revelation of his love as I submitted. He navigated and continued to steer my life according to his will. He strengthened me, took my shame, healed, and restored me. My relationship with Jesus is so much deeper today.

Tracy's Glass's devotionals are a reminder of who God wants to be in every season of your life. Her words encourage you to trust God to navigate you to the other side of the shore. Tracy's words, inspired by the Holy Spirit, will comfort, encourage, and deliver. These devotionals are a steppingstone and road map into the daily presence and communion with Jesus."

—Reverend Vickie Douglas

"When life hits hard and restoration seems impossible it's the promises of God that provides us with hope. Tracy Glass's thirty-day offering of *Restored* invites us on a journey to move beyond despair to living an amazing life of grace anchored in God's truth. *Restored* is a beautiful resource to help women discover true hope beyond their hurt."

—Linda Goldfarb
Award-winning author and podcaster,
and board-certified Christian life coach

"In the toughest days of my difficult divorce, I clung to the wise and hopeful words of women who were on the other side of my valley. Tracy Glass is one of these women. In this book, she shares encouraging stories to help lift you from the pit of discouragement. The promises of scripture and grace to rebuild section are especially helpful for reframing your perspective. *Restored* will be a lifeline in your time of desperate need."

—Sarah Geringer
Christian author, speaker, artist, editor,
book launch manager, and creative coach

"I echo the words found written within this encouraging book by Tracy Glass: 'Restored is so much more than words written on a page. It's a heartfelt hug.' Tracy gets you. Mixed with transparency, prayer, life-changing scripture, and a gentle spirit, she holds your hand through the pages as you journey through the road to restoration. Start reading it today!"

—Courtnaye Richard
Author of *IDENTIFIED*
and Founder of Inside Out with Courtnaye

"*Restored* is a loving, insightful guide, prayerfully created to facilitate healing. Tracy has walked the path and triumphantly emerged from the heartbreaking experience of divorce. Because of that, she can firmly and faithfully provide devotionals that can help other women navigate their journey without getting stuck in the pain pitfalls that prevent some from fulfilling their destiny. This book is a treasure."

—Janice Edwards
Award-wining talk show host,
Emmy-nominated producer, businessowner, minister

TRACY GLASS

RESTORED

God's Promises to Beautifully Rebuild
You After Divorce or Separation

RESTORED

God's Promises To Beautifully Rebuild You After Divorce or Separation

TRACY GLASS

Abundance Books

Published by Abundance Books, LLC, Kalamazoo, MI
abundance-books.com

ISBN: 978-1-963377-40-8 (paperback)
ISBN: 978-1-963377-41-5 (ebook)

Published in the United States of America.

10 9 8 7 6 5 4 3 2 1

Author represented by AuthorizeMe Literary Firm, Sharon Elliott, Agent, AuthorizeMe.net
Edited by Larry J. Leech II
Cover Design by Amber Wiegand-Buckley, Barefaced Media
Interior design by WendyEL Creative

*For every woman whose spirit breaks under the
weight of a fractured relationship
and broken dreams.
This book is for you.*

CONTENTS

 INTRODUCTION

Dear Friend,

I know firsthand how devastating life can be when your world is shattered by separation or divorce. The agonizing pain, the relentless questions of self-worth, the fear of an uncertain future. I've been there.

During my healing journey, I longed for a compassionate voice to comfort my aching soul and guide me back to wholeness. I poured my heart into creating *Restored,* so you don't have to walk this difficult road alone.

This 30-day devotional is my labor of love, designed to nurture your spirit with tenderness and God's truth as you navigate the turmoil. Each day, you'll find a reading to embrace your grief while rediscovering the courage to keep moving forward. Through personal stories that mirror your own, uplifting scriptures, soul-stirring reflections, and intimate prayers, you will be encouraged to trust God in your healing process.

Whether wrestling with loss, betrayal, or insecurities, these pages will breathe life into you. They will remind you that you are cherished, worthy, and never abandoned by your Heavenly Father.

Restored is so much more than words on a page. It's a heartfelt hug, capturing the profound comfort and kindness I experienced through Christ while I walked my path to healing. Writing this was my way of offering you a soothing touch while possibly sparking hope and reawaken a sense of purpose as you heal.

I can't promise the path will be easy. But I can assure you that with Scripture as your compass and honesty as your guide, you will rediscover the unshakable truth and restoration power of understanding who you are in Christ.

Take my hand, and let's walk this journey toward renewal together, one courageous step at a time.

TRACY

 PART 1

HOPE DURING UNCERTAINTY

Don't worry about anything; instead, pray about everything. Tell God what you need, and thank him for all he has done. Then you will experience God's peace, which exceeds anything we can understand. His peace will guard your hearts and minds as you live in Christ Jesus (Philippians 4:6-7)

RUNNING FROM THE MESS

The angel of the LORD found Hagar beside a spring of water in the wilderness, along the road to Shur. The angel said to her, 'Hagar, Sarai's servant, where have you come from, and where are you going?' 'I'm running away from my mistress, Sarai,' she replied. (Genesis 16:7-8)

Sometimes, the most attractive solution to a problem or uncomfortable situation is to escape. For example, when walking through my divorce, I frequently said, "I just want to run away." Unfortunately, when reality set in and I realized the many responsibilities and people depending on me—children, car and mortgage payments, and other commitments—the dream of my great escape became a fleeting thought.

Navigating through separation and a divorce can feel like an endless nightmare. A significant part of my healing journey was to acknowledge and embrace the intense feelings and challenges that come with separation and divorce rather than try to flee from them.

Ignoring those legal documents, pretending the betrayal didn't happen, or minimizing the pain didn't make my heartache and despair disappear. While pretending could be a short-term way to deal with the suffering, it's not the long-term healing strategy God has in mind. He has a way of derailing our plans to escape.

In Genesis 16, Hagar, Sarah's servant, decides to run away because her situation takes an unexpected detour when she becomes the solution to Abraham and Sarah's infertility problem. Hagar became Abraham's second wife and got pregnant, and her relationship with her mistress became complicated. The tension caused her tremendous emotional pain, including rejection, betrayal, abandonment, and fear. Even though the mess Hagar endured was not all her fault, God was still faithful to Hagar and blessed her despite it all.

In verses 9-13, Hagar receives a powerful promise from God through an angel. He saw the messy situation and had a better escape plan than her plan of not facing the mess. Hagar learned to trust God to receive his promised blessing. But before trust came, she needed to face her fears, learn how to navigate uncomfortable situations, and swallow her pride.

Like he did with Hagar, God will empower you to face the mess your separation or divorce is causing, even as you process and walk through it. He has a beautiful restorative plan designed just for you. Hagar's courage and the blessings God provided for her throughout her life can encourage us to trust him as we face our messy moments.

SCRIPTURES ABOUT HAGAR

> **GENESIS 16:1-3:** "Now Sarai, Abram's wife, had not been able to bear children for him. But she had an Egyptian servant named Hagar. So Sarai said to Abram, 'The LORD has prevented me from having children. Go and sleep with my servant. Perhaps I can have children through her.' And Abram agreed with Sarai's proposal. So Sarai, Abram's wife, took Hagar the Egyptian servant and gave her to Abram as a wife." (This happened ten years after Abram had settled in the land of Canaan.)

GENESIS 16:4-6: "So Abram had sexual relations with Hagar, and she became pregnant. But when Hagar knew she was pregnant, she began to treat her mistress, Sarai, with contempt. Then Sarai said to Abram, 'This is all your fault! I put my servant into your arms, but now that she's pregnant she treats me with contempt. The LORD will show who's wrong—you or me!' Abram replied, 'Look, she is your servant, so deal with her as you see fit.' Then Sarai treated Hagar so harshly that she finally ran away."

GENESIS 16:10-14: "Then he added, 'I will give you more descendants than you can count.' And the angel also said, 'You are now pregnant and will give birth to a son. You are to name him Ishmael (which means 'God hears'), for the LORD has heard your cry of distress. This son of yours will be a wild man, as untamed as a wild donkey! He will raise his fist against everyone, and everyone will be against him. Yes, he will live in open hostility against all his relatives.' Thereafter, Hagar used another name to refer to the LORD, who had spoken to her. She said, 'You are the God who sees me.' She also said, 'Have I truly seen the One who sees me?' So that well was named Beer-lahai-roi (which means 'well of the Living One who sees me'). It can still be found between Kadesh and Bered."

PROMISES DURING MESSY TIMES

PROMISE OF GUIDANCE. JOHN 8:12: "Jesus spoke to the people once more and said, 'I am the light of the world. If you follow me, you won't have to walk in darkness, because you will have the light that leads to life.'"

PROMISE OF POWER AND STRENGTH. ISAIAH 40:29-31: "He gives power to the weak and strength to the powerless. Even youths will become weak and tired, and young men will fall in exhaustion. But those who trust in the LORD will find new strength. They will soar high on wings like eagles. They will run and not grow weary. They will walk and not faint."

PROMISE OF PEACE. PHILIPPIANS 4:6-7: "Don't worry about anything; instead pray about everything. Tell God what you need, and thank him for all he has done. Then you will experience God's peace, which exceeds anything we can understand. His peace will guard your hearts and minds as you live in Christ Jesus."

GRACE TO REBUILD

Take a moment and think about a specific situation during your separation or divorce that pulled you toward the urge to escape. What was your immediate reaction? What emotions did you face, and how did you handle them?

Think about Hagar's story in Genesis 16. It's a reminder of how God sticks with us through all the messy stuff in life. What lessons can you take from Hagar's journey—her trust and courage when dealing with her challenges? How do you think you can use her experiences to find hope and cling to God's promises of restoration for you?

God made specific promises to Hagar in chapters 16:9–10 and 21:17–18. What promises has he given you that give you hope and a sense of restoration in your situation? Jot down those promises and how they can be your guiding light, shaping how you see things and your actions during your separation or divorce.

PRAYER

Dear Heavenly Father, I am coming to you today with a heavy heart. I am struggling with the emotional trauma and drama of my broken relationship. I feel lost. I don't know how to pick up the pieces and move on. Although I want to run away, I know that with your help, I can get through this. I trust you have a restoration promise and plan for me, and you see me and will never leave or forsake me.

As David wrote in Psalm 40, you have heard my cry and are lifting me out of my pit of despair. You set my feet on solid ground and steadied me as I walked along. I can't wait to get to the other side of this mess. I often think about the new things waiting for me. I want to dream, sing, dance, and be free again. One day, I know this challenging season will become a powerful testimony for others to witness the hope you offer when we go through messy situations. In Jesus's name, I pray. Amen.

YOU'RE MORE VALUABLE THAN YOU THINK

But the LORD said to Samuel, 'Don't judge by his appearance or height, for I have rejected him. The LORD doesn't see things the way you see them. People judge by outward appearance, but the LORD looks at the heart.' (1 Samuel 16:7)

After neglecting my BBQ smoker for more than eight years, it had become a sorry sight. Faded, rusted, and weighing a hefty 300 pounds, the smoker had seen better days. The inside was coated with baked-on grime, mold, and other unsavory substances.

I tried to find a new home for my outdoor oven, but no one was interested in taking this ugly piece of junk off my hands. With no takers, I decided to dispose of the smoker at the dump. I made plans for the smoker to be hauled away, but on the scheduled day, I received a text message canceling the pickup. Frustration washed over me when I realized I couldn't get rid of this eyesore.

A week later, during a visit from my professional BBQ enthusiast friend, I mentioned my plan to get rid of my neglected smoker. To my surprise, he advised me not to give it away. He educated me about the value of my equipment by explaining that despite its cosmetic flaws, this was a relic with a solid foundation and could be easily restored at a minimal cost. He even generously offered to help me fix the unit.

Inspired by my friend's expertise and guidance, we dove into the two-week restoration project with enthusiasm. We rolled up our sleeves and worked tirelessly, repairing the smoker, and giving it a fresh makeover. Bit by bit, the smoker began to regain its former glory until, finally, looking almost as good as new.

While I admired the beautifully restored BBQ project, I couldn't help but draw parallels to my life. Like the smoker, I had experienced my fair share of wear and tear over the years, and my value may not have been apparent to others and myself at times. However, through this restoration process, I learned a valuable lesson about God's restorative plan for my life.

Just as my friend saw the hidden potential in the worn-out smoker and helped restore it to its former greatness, I realized God sees the same in me. Despite my imperfections and past mistakes, he plans to restore and renew me, to bring out my true value and potential. This experience was a powerful reminder not to judge a book by its cover but to trust in the restorative power of God's love and grace in my life.

After restoring the smoker, I gleaned some truths about God's restorative plan for my life:

⇛ God sees beyond my flaws and faults and recognizes my true potential. I need to surround myself with people who also see my value and encourage my potential, lift me, and support me.

⇛ Because something looks worn down doesn't mean it's not worth restoring. I must continue to believe in God's ability to restore the areas of my life that feel lost or stolen. It's crucial not to lose hope prematurely, even when the storms of life have left me feeling beaten up, and my dreams and goals may seem rusty and faded.

℘ The restoration process takes time, effort, and hard work. I need to invest the time and energy to sand off the rust and clean up the ugliness in my life. Restoration may require using high-powered tools to tackle deeper issues beyond the surface level, but with perseverance and determination, I can make progress.

Just like restoring an old, rusty smoker, the process of your restoration may also come with challenges. Don't give up. Be willing to put in the hard work, use the right tools, and take the time needed to bring out the true beauty and potential in your life. When God steps into our circumstances, he gives us spiritual eyes to see ourselves in a new light. We begin to see our true worth and value, and we realize that our past experiences or failures do not define our identity. With God's guidance and grace, we can emerge from the restoration process stronger, wiser, and with a renewed sense of purpose.

SCRIPTURES ABOUT HOW GOD SEES OUR VALUE

EPHESIANS 2:10: "For we are God's masterpiece. He has created us anew in Christ Jesus, so we can do the good things he planned for us long ago."

LUKE 1:45: "You are blessed because you believed that the Lord would do what he said."

1 PETER 5:10: "In his kindness God called you to share in his eternal glory by means of Christ Jesus. So after you have suffered a little while, he will restore, support, and strengthen you, and he will place you on a firm foundation."

PROMISES FOR RENEWAL AND RESTORATION

PROMISE OF SOARING. ISAIAH 40:31: "But those who trust in the LORD will find new strength. They will soar high on wings like eagles. They will run and not grow weary. They will walk and not faint."

PROMISE OF COMFORT. ISAIAH 41:10: "Don't be afraid, for I am with you. Don't be discouraged, for I am your God. I will strengthen you and help you. I will hold you up with my victorious right hand."

PROMISE OF BLESSINGS. ISAIAH 61:3: "To all who mourn in Israel, he will give a crown of beauty for ashes, a joyous blessing instead of mourning, festive praise instead of despair. In their righteousness, they will be like great oaks that the LORD has planted for his own glory."

GRACE TO REBUILD

Has your separation or divorce made you feel like that old BBQ smoker? Your true value and potential hidden beneath the surface, maybe not so apparent to others or even to yourself. How has this experience made you feel, and have you learned any valuable lessons from it?

_____

_____

_____

Think about the friend who saw the hidden potential in the smoker and offered support in restoring it. How crucial is it to have people around who see your true worth and push you toward your full potential? How can you build and nurture relationships that lift you up and provide the support you need on this journey?

_____

_____

_____

Have you ever thought about how you see yourself through God's eyes, recognizing your real worth and value the way he does. How has your past experiences and mistakes shaped your identity? How can you embrace the idea that restoration boosts your potential and worth?

_____

_____

_____

PRAYER

Dear Heavenly Father, thank you for your presence during this difficult time. I'm reassured that you see my potential, and soon, I will see the same things you see. I can get through each day because of your love and grace. I am so grateful for your promises of healing and restoration. I know you are faithful and will lead me to a place of peace even when I question my value. I don't know my future, and trusting your restoration process is hard. Help me build my trust in you so I can fully trust your timing and know you will work everything out for my good. In Jesus's name, I pray. Amen.

SHUTTING OFF THE NOISE

But when you pray, go away by yourself, shut the door behind you, and pray to your Father in private. Then your Father, who sees everything, will reward you. (Matthew 6:6)

You know, amidst all the noise surrounding us, the accusations, and the attacks, it's easy to feel overwhelmed. We want to hit the mute button on life but are sometimes unsure how. Well, here's the thing: God's got a secret place just for us. This spot is for us and him, away from all the noise and distractions. In this place, we can take a break from all the chaos, find rest, and rediscover the rhythm of our lives.

God reminds us of our true worth and value in this sacred place. It's also where we can find peace, healing, and a fresh sense of purpose. We can be still, listen to God's voice, and remember that we are cherished children of God, deserving of love and grace. So, let's take refuge in his presence, silence the noise, and let him restore and guide us toward a brighter future. Just imagine God saying this to you:

"Let's create a secret place for us. I'll meet you there, offering rest, peace, and everything you need. You can make it special and choose the place—a room, a closet, your car, the park, or even the floor. I'll be waiting, ready to hear you out. I love being invited into your secret place! You don't need fancy words; a simple request for my presence works. I only ask two things:

1. Don't hesitate to come to me, even if you feel unworthy or unsure.

2. Turn off all distractions before we chat. Our secret place is where we'll connect deeply. I want to share some amazing things with you. 1 Corinthians 2:9 says, 'No eye has seen, no ear has heard, and mind has imagined what I have prepared for those who love me.' When you pray to me in secret, I will see and hear only you. The rewards you'll obtain won't be hidden, but you and others will witness you becoming a strong rock connected to me, empowering you to overcome anything."

SCRIPTURES ABOUT CONNECTING WITH GOD IN THE SECRET PLACE

PSALM 91:3: "For he will rescue you from every trap and protect you from deadly disease."

ISAIAH 30:15: "This is what the Sovereign LORD, the Holy One of Israel, says: 'Only in returning to me and resting in me will you be saved. In quietness and confidence is your strength. But you would have none of it.'"

MATTHEW 6:6: "But when you pray, go away by yourself, shut the door behind you, and pray to your Father in private. Then your Father, who sees everything, will reward you."

PROMISES IN THE SECRET PLACE

PROMISE OF SAFETY AND REST. PSALM 91:1-2: "Those who live in the shelter of the Most High will find rest in the shadow of the Almighty. This I declare about the LORD: He alone is my refuge, my place of safety; he is my God, and I trust him."

PROMISE OF CONCEALMENT AND PROTECTION. PSALM 27:5: "For he will conceal me there when troubles come; he will hide me in his sanctuary. He will place me out of reach on a high rock."

PROMISE OF GOODNESS. PSALM 31:19-20: "How great is the goodness you have stored up for those who fear you. You lavish it on those who come to you for protection, blessing them before the watching world. You hide them in the shelter of your presence, safe from those who conspire against them. You shelter them in your presence, far from accusing tongues."

GRACE TO REBUILD

Designing a personal space for your communion with God can be incredibly life-giving. If you have already created such a space, what aspects make it special to you? If you haven't yet, think about how you can tailor this space to reflect your personality and make it welcoming for your moments with God. It could be as simple as dedicating your favorite chair, a corner of your bedroom, or a spot in your garden for this purpose.

_____

_____

_____

Consider the obstacles that disrupt your connection with God. Identify the primary sources of these distractions. How can you effectively eliminate these interruptions during your moments of prayer? For instance, you might hang a sign on the door indicating "Mommy Time" or "Talking to God, please do not disturb" to ensure uninterrupted privacy.

_____

_____

_____

Picture meeting with God in your secret place. What would you tell him? What would you want to hear from him? How could this encounter bring you rest and guidance?

_____

_____

_____

PRAYER

Dear Heavenly Father, I ask you to silence the voice of the enemy. Please help me to hear your voice above all others, clear and powerful. Fill my mind with thoughts of good memories and the bright future you have planned for me. I am excited to walk into your perfect plans for my life, knowing you have good things in store for me. Thank you for your guidance and protection. In Jesus's name, I pray. Amen.

HOW DID THIS HAPPEN?

All who fear the LORD will hate evil. Therefore, I hate pride and arrogance, corruption, and perverse speech. (Proverbs 8:13)

Reflecting on my divorce, I often find myself pondering over how the marriage all came apart, how a bond I believed was unbreakable could simply crumble into nothingness. At the core of this shattered relationship was pride—stubborn desires to always be right, to control, to come out on top. In the end, it was selfishness that stood at the heart of our broken relationship.

According to the Bible, Satan, once described as the model of perfection, ultimately embraced evil. His character shifted from perfect to evil due to his pride and desire for power, leading God to cast him out of heaven and impose a death sentence on him.

In a message sent to the Prince of Tyre (interpreted as Satan) in Ezekiel 28:11-19 (MSG), God provides insight into the reasons behind Satan's fall from grace:

Satan was adorned with splendor and positioned as an anointed cherub in Eden. He embodied perfection. However, pride led to his downfall. His misuse of wisdom for personal gain and corrupt actions resulted in violence and sin, prompting his expulsion from God's presence. Ultimately, Satan's once magnificent form was reduced to ashes, a testament to the consequences of pride and corruption.

Pride led to Satan's expulsion from heaven and often sits at the heart of marital breakdowns. Recognizing pride can be discerned through phrases such as "I need," "I deserve," or "I desire." Given pride's ability to dethrone an anointed cherub, it's crucial for us to be vigilant in not harboring pride within ourselves.

Pride manifests itself when we think we are above obedience to God's Word, live independently from him, or become unsatisfied with his blessings. Satan took his position in heaven for granted and lost everything. The antidote to pride is humility.

Humility prioritizes not what I need and deserve but what God thinks and deserves. The difference between pride and humility becomes clear when facing challenging situations. Pride tends to resist and blame others, while humility seeks unity and values the opinions of others. Despite the difficulties arising when a relationship fractures, it is crucial to strive for humility.

Consider trying a more humble approach when faced with situations tempting a prideful response. This might involve pausing to view the situation objectively, demonstrating empathy and understanding, and considering the needs and feelings of all involved. This way, you might find solutions that work for everyone rather than just pushing your way. Instead of rushing to get what you want, take the time to listen to the other person's point of view and aim for a win-win solution. Listening and pursuing peace always leads to a much better outcome.

SCRIPTURES ABOUT PRIDE VS. HUMILITY

PROVERBS 11:2: "Pride leads to disgrace, but with humility comes wisdom."

PROVERBS 15:33: "Fear of the LORD teaches wisdom; humility precedes honor."

PROVERBS 18:12: "Haughtiness goes before destruction; humility precedes honor."

PROMISES WHEN WE EMBRACE HUMILITY

PROMISE OF ACCEPTANCE. PSALM 51:17: "The sacrifice you desire is a broken spirit. You will not reject a broken and repentant heart, O God."

PROMISE OF HEALING. 2 CHRONICLES 7:14: "Then if my people who are called by my name will humble themselves and pray and seek my face and turn from their wicked ways, I will hear from heaven and will forgive their sins and restore their land."

PROMISE OF SUPPORT. PSALM 147:6: "The LORD supports the humble, but he brings the wicked down into the dust."

GRACE TO REBUILD

Have you ever found yourself exhibiting excessive pride or arrogance in your thoughts or actions? How did those moments unfold, and what were the repercussions on your relationships or decision-making?

_____

_____

_____

Reflect on instances when you consciously chose humility over pride, even when you knew or thought you knew the best option or correct answer. What were the outcomes of those moments?

_____

_____

_____

Consider a recent challenging situation. Reflect on your initial reaction and assess whether pride played a role. Envision addressing a similar situation with a humbler attitude. What steps can you take to prioritize humility, seek to understand others, and devise solutions that benefit all parties involved?

_____

_____

_____

PRAYER

Dear Heavenly Father, I am so thankful for your love. I know you are with me even when I have a negative attitude about my broken relationship and don't have any good thoughts about my spouse or ex-spouse. Despite the unfairness and every emotion I am experiencing now, you desire me to seek your opinions on everything. God, what are your thoughts? Please help me eliminate any pride. I know you are faithful and will see me through this season. I cling to your promises and pray for your strength and peace. In Jesus's name, I pray. Amen.

COVER ALL ACCESS POINTS

But when I am afraid, I will put my trust in you. I praise God for what he has promised. I trust in God, so why should I be afraid? What can mere mortals do to me? (Psalm 56:3-4)

I used to harbor a fear that I was too embarrassed to talk about openly. But I've decided to share now because I've worked through it, and I hope my story can encourage others.

One morning, a mouse scurried out from under my bed. Encountering a mouse has always been one of my biggest fears and seeing one in my bedroom worsened matters. The tiny rodent disrupted my life, forcing me to move out of my bedroom, spend money on traps, and even hire a pest control company. I found myself tiptoeing around my house, holding my breath, being constantly on edge, and fearing the mouse would appear at any moment, surprising me with a "Boo!"

Eventually, the little mouse got caught, and my house was cleared of him and all evidence of his visit, but I was still mortified. Weeks later, the Lord asked me a simple question: "When will you move back into your room?" I said, "I'm not sure." But he assured me I didn't have to worry about the mouse. Reflecting on my reaction to the mouse, I realized some important things about fear:

TRUE FREEDOM COMES THROUGH FACING FEAR: I confronted my fear head-on when I came face-to-face with the mouse. I caught it on a sticky trap by the tail, but my attempt to use bug spray to drown it only made it struggle harder. The mouse broke free from the trap and ran into an opening in my cabinet. I discovered his hiding place.

UNCOVER THE ENTRY POINTS OF FEAR: Seeing the mouse escape into the cabinet upset me, so I turned to the Lord for guidance. He told me to cover all access points. I sealed off garage doors, cracks, and cabinets to prevent further entry.

OVERCOMING FEAR IS POSSIBLE: I realized my fear was based on false assumptions. There had been no evidence of a mouse in my home for weeks. With renewed trust in the Lord's protection, I finally moved back into my room, taking a step of faith despite my lingering fear.

Have faith because God cares about every aspect of your life, including the things you may be hesitant to discuss, such as your broken relationship. You can approach God, your loving Father, who will provide you the courage to confront and overcome your greatest fear. Trust in his unwavering support and guidance as you navigate through this challenging time in your life.

SCRIPTURES ABOUT GOD'S PROTECTION IN MOMENTS OF FEAR

2 TIMOTHY 1:7: "For God has not given us a spirit of fear and timidity, but of power, love, and self-discipline."

PSALM 56:3: "But when I am afraid, I will put my trust in you."

PSALM 27:1: "The LORD is my light and my salvation—so why should I be afraid? The LORD is my fortress, protecting me from danger, so why should I tremble?"

PROMISES WHEN WE FACE FEAR

PROMISE OF PEACE. JOHN 14:27: "I am leaving you with a gift—peace of mind and heart. And the peace I give is a gift the world cannot give. So don't be troubled or afraid."

PROMISE OF LOVE. 1 JOHN 4:18: "Such love has no fear because perfect love expels all fear. If we are afraid, it is for fear of punishment, and this shows that we have not fully experienced his perfect love."

PROMISE OF ASSURANCE. PROVERBS 29:25: "Fearing people is a dangerous trap, but trusting the LORD means safety."

GRACE TO REBUILD

Take a moment to look back on the past week and jot down five things you're thankful for. Big or small, how did these blessings affect your week, mood, or relationships? Expressing gratitude can totally shift your focus to the positive aspects in your life.

_____

_____

_____

Think about a recent challenge you faced. Describe the situation, your initial feelings, and the steps you took to conquer it. What did you learn, and how did it shape your personal growth and resilience?

_____

_____

_____

Write a letter to your future self—could be a year from now or even longer. Share your current hopes, dreams, and goals. Paint a picture of the person you want to become. What steps are you planning to take to get there?

_____

_____

_____

PRAYER

Dear Heavenly Father, I pray for your guidance. I desire to close any access points I have unknowingly opened, allowing the enemy access to the negative emotions I am currently processing. Give me wisdom and discernment to identify these access points, whether from past wounds, unforgiveness, unhealthy thought patterns, or areas where I have not fully surrendered to your will. Help me identify where the enemy has gained a foothold in my heart and mind. Help me take the necessary steps to close these access points. Please guide me in healing from past wounds and replacing negative thought patterns with your truth and promises. Thank you for personally being with me on my healing journey. In Jesus's name, I pray. Amen.

PART 2

HOPE FOR THE FUTURE

I pray that God, the source of hope, will fill you completely with joy and peace because you trust in him. Then you will overflow with confident hope through the power of the Holy Spirit. (Romans 15:13)

FROM HOPELESSNESS TO HOPE

"For I know the plans I have for you," says the LORD.
"They are plans for good and not for disaster, to give
you a future and a hope." (Jeremiah 29:11)

In a world where convenience and instant gratification are valued, seeking fulfillment in temporary solutions is expected. Have you observed the growing trend of people turning to platforms like Amazon for shopping?

Shopping on Amazon is convenient, but it also meets an emotional need. I'll admit, I rush to the door when I receive the notification letting me know my package has arrived. The anticipation of ripping open the box is exciting. Although I love to shop, the experience fails to address my more profound need for lasting and fulfilling hope.

Life's challenges can lead us to experience hopelessness and prompt us to question the purpose and significance of our struggles. During a season of intense emotional pain, I asked God, "What good can this ugliness produce? How can I give you glory when I'm overwhelmed with disappointment and sadness?" During relational challenges, it becomes crucial to discover a sustainable source of hope. An uplifting and strengthening hope will help us rebuild our lives. This type of hope is an invaluable and beautiful gift.

The solution to hopelessness is found in Scripture. We are encouraged to trust God, the ultimate source of hope. He understands our deepest needs and can grant us renewed hope, joy, and peace when we trust him. Romans 15:13 reminds us of this truth—while we trust in the God of hope, we are filled with overflowing joy and peace by the power of the Holy Spirit.

We can find comfort in the promise of a bright future which God has planned for us. Knowing our present circumstances do not determine our final destiny is reassuring. God is faithful and true to his Word. He declares in Jeremiah 29:11, he knows the plans he has for us—plans for peace, not evil, to give us a future and hope.

God is our promise-keeper. Even in our darkest moments, we can trust His faithfulness because he stands firm on every promise in Scripture. He is our guiding light, a beacon of hope, leading us out of darkness and reminding us that his intentions toward us are always good. The journey from hopelessness to hope requires us to trust in God, who holds our future in his hands. The temporary pleasures of this world cannot compare to the enduring hope God provides.

During desperation, we can turn to God, seek his guidance, and find sustainable excitement and anticipation about his good plans for our future. His plans for us surpass our limited understanding of what we face now. God's plans have possibilities and blessings beyond our imagination. Embrace new hope—God is our promise keeper and faithful to complete the good work he has started in us.

SCRIPTURES ABOUT GOD'S PROMISES
FOR OUR FUTURE

PHILIPPIANS 1:6: "And I am certain that God, who began the good work within you, will continue his work until it is finally finished on the day when Christ Jesus returns."

2 CORINTHIANS 4:17: "For our present troubles are small and won't last very long. Yet they produce for us a glory that vastly outweighs them and will last forever!"

EPHESIANS 2:10: "For we are God's masterpiece. He has created us anew in Christ Jesus, so we can do the good things he planned for us long ago."

PROMISES WHEN WE FEEL HOPELESS

PROMISE OF RESTORATION. JOEL 2:25: "The LORD says, 'I will give you back what you lost to the swarming locusts, the hopping locusts, the stripping locusts, and the cutting locusts. It was I who sent this great destroying army against you.'"

PROMISE OF GOD HEARING. PSALM 34:17-18: "The LORD hears his people when they call to him for help. He rescues them from all their troubles. The LORD is close to the brokenhearted; he rescues those whose spirits are crushed."

PROMISE OF COMFORT. ISAIAH 61:1-3: "The Spirit of the Sovereign LORD is upon me, for the LORD has anointed me to bring good news to the poor. He has sent me to comfort the brokenhearted and to proclaim that captives will be released, and prisoners will be freed. He has sent me to tell those who mourn that the time of the LORD's favor has come and with it, the day of God's anger against their enemies. To all who mourn in Israel, he will give a crown of beauty for ashes, a joyous blessing instead of mourning, festive praise instead of despair. In their righteousness, they will be like great oaks that the LORD has planted for his own glory."

GRACE TO REBUILD

How can you confront and change any negative beliefs that are getting in the way of your hope?

_____

_____

_____

What practical things can you do to take care of yourself—body, emotions, and spirit—to boost your hope?

_____

_____

_____

Who are your go-to people for support and motivation? How can they be your partners in rebuilding?

_____

_____

_____

PRAYER

Dear Heavenly Father, I can turn to you in times of hopelessness because you are the source of all hope. I trust you. You understand my needs and can grant me renewed hope, joy, and peace. Please help me to hold onto your promises, especially when life feels overwhelming. I desire to find comfort in your plan for my future, knowing your intentions for me are good and purposeful. Strengthen my faith and guide me as I navigate through some overwhelming challenges. In Jesus's name, I pray. Amen.

DAY 7

WHAT ARE GOD'S PLANS?

You can make many plans, but the LORD's
purpose will prevail. (Proverbs 19:21)

What are God's plans for my life? That's a question many of us have asked at some point. There was a time when I thought I had my life all figured out. I could whip out a PowerPoint presentation with graphics and animations, give a riveting motivational speech about my five-year plan and convince others to join me.

Elaborate plans and dreams of success filled my mind, but everything changed after the divorce. I believed my plans aligned with God's, but I came to understand I had strayed from his path. The goals and dreams I chased left me feeling empty, always pursuing moving targets. This realization led me to a couple of truths, profoundly shifting my perspective:

ϡ My plans were not in alignment with God's plans. I needed to seek his direction rather than rely solely on my desires. I understood the only endeavors that genuinely matter and bring lasting impact and satisfaction are those pursued for the glory of Christ.

ϡ God revealed he was sovereign—the leader, teacher, forgiver, and Savior who can change my circumstances however and whenever he pleases. God controls my life.

These realizations redirected my focus from self-centered ambitions to God-focused ambitions. Now, my heart desires to accomplish things that align with God's purposes, to make a positive impact in the lives of others, and to seek his guidance in every step consistently. I have found that true satisfaction comes not from pursuing my agenda but from surrendering to God's will and trusting in his good plans for my life.

I've been humbled to discover that God's plans surpass my own. God has shown me my plans are small compared to his big blueprint for my life. When I stepped aside and allowed God to have control, I witnessed how he turned court decisions in my favor and blessed me with a financial increase. He can turn an impossible situation into something possible.

If you're feeling stuck or unfulfilled, I want to encourage you not to dismiss those feelings. The Holy Spirit is drawing you and wanting to lead you into a closer relationship with Jesus. It may be time to shift your focus to discovering God's new plans. You may want to set aside some of your ambitions and spend more time seeking God about your next steps. Begin by acknowledging Jesus as Lord, repenting of your sins, and inviting him into your heart.

When we invite someone into our hearts, we make room for them. We prioritize their desires and value their opinions. In the same way, when we invite Jesus into our lives, we open ourselves up to his leading and allow him to shape our plans and purposes. So, while we ponder God's plans for our lives, we realize they can be discovered when we prioritize and trust him 100 percent even when it doesn't make sense, and when we seek his will above our own. Then, he will guide us on his path—a journey filled with purpose, fulfillment, and intimacy with Jesus.

SCRIPTURES ABOUT GOD'S PLANS

PROVERBS 16:9: "We can make our plans, but the LORD determines our steps."

PSALM 138:8: "The LORD will work out his plans for my life—for your faithful love, O LORD, endures forever. Don't abandon me, for you made me."

PROVERBS 3:5-6: "Trust in the LORD with all your heart; do not depend on your own understanding. Seek his will in all you do, and he will show you which path to take."

PROMISES OF GOD'S PLANS

PROMISE OF REFRESHING. ISAIAH 58:11: "The LORD will guide you continually, giving you water when you are dry and restoring your strength. You will be like a well-watered garden, like an ever-flowing spring."

PROMISE TO WATCH OVER US. PSALM 32:8: "The LORD says, 'I will guide you along the best pathway for your life. I will advise you and watch over you.'"

PROMISE TO TEACH US. PSALM 25:4-5: "Show me the right path, O LORD; point out the road for me to follow. Lead me by your truth and teach me, for you are the God who saves me. All day long I put my hope in you."

GRACE TO REBUILD

Take a moment to write down what you're currently chasing—your goals, dreams, and aspirations in this life journey of yours.

_____

_____

_____

Think about how these ambitions can sync up with God's will. Any changes, shifts in perspective, or new directions you might need to explore to align with his purpose for your life?

_____

_____

_____

What practical steps can you add to your daily routine to make seeking God's guidance a priority?

_____

_____

_____

PRAYER

Dear Heavenly Father, I come before you with a humble heart, seeking guidance and wisdom as I discover your plans for my life. I acknowledge that there are areas in my life where I need healing, restoration, and transformation to walk fully in your perfect plans. Please reveal any areas of fear, doubt, or unbelief that may hinder me from embracing your new plans for me. Thank you for your promise to guide me to your perfect plans for my life. In Jesus's name, I pray. Amen.

DAY 8

STEPPING BEYOND SAFE PLACES

The LORD is my rock, my fortress, and my savior; my God is my rock, in whom I find protection. He is my shield, the power that saves me, and my place of safety. (Psalm 18:2)

In the season of divorce, I discovered a valuable lesson about the importance of feeling emotionally safe. The separation and divorce process can leave you feeling hyper-vigilant, constantly on guard, and trying to decipher the motives of even your loved ones.

The absence of safety can lead you to seek comfort, even if it means returning to a painful situation. The predictability of pain can appear more secure than the unpredictable feeling of being unsafe. Predictability became synonymous with safety, and I would go to great lengths to find a sense of security, even if it meant isolating myself.

I heard a story about a man with bent legs who relied on a skateboard to navigate his way. Every day, he would be found on street corners, begging for money. One day, an orthopedic surgeon noticed and told the man that he could fix his legs and restore his mobility, all at no cost. The surgeon offered the man the opportunity for healing and freedom through surgery.

The paralyzed man agreed to the surgery. However, on the day of the procedure, he was nowhere to be found. A month later, he was spotted in another city, still begging, with no signs of change.

Why would he run away when guaranteed healing and freedom were within reach? We can only speculate about the reasons behind the man's decision. Possibly, his mind was trapped in a state of predictability. He struggled to envision a life beyond begging because being unhoused had become his haven—a place of familiarity and security.

Similarly, I found myself relating to the paralyzed man's situation. I had grown comfortable with the routine of coming home and retreating to the safety of my bedroom. Although I could imagine a better life, fear kept me from stepping out of my comfort zone and venturing into the unknown.

Both the paralyzed man and I faced the challenge of breaking free from the limitations imposed by our safe places. We longed for change and improvement, but fear became a barrier to transformation. I realized my benchmark for safety needed to shift. While feeling safe remained non-negotiable, I understood that predictability alone should not determine my sense of security.

Relying solely on predictability made me risk averse. I became afraid to walk through the new doors God was opening, meet the people whom he sent to help me, or seek guidance from trained counselors who could lead me to emotional safety. Running away from open doors and remaining complacent in my comfort zone hindered me from experiencing the abundant life God had in store for me.

Through prayer and counseling, I understood the need to confront fear, even beyond my divorce healing process. But I also discovered God understood my fears and desires. He longed to guide me toward a life beyond the boundaries of my safe places. The sweetest fruit is found at the top of the tree, and we must climb higher and reach farther to harvest it. In the same way, we must rise higher and go farther than our comfort zones to taste the sweetness of life.

Remember, God is with you, offering his protection, strength, and guidance. With his presence, you can safely step beyond your safe places and venture into the unknown with courage and faith. Embrace the abundant life he has prepared for you beyond what you can see or control. Trust he will be your rock, fortress, and place of safety as you journey into the extraordinary plans he has for you.

SCRIPTURES ABOUT STEPPING OUT OF OUR COMFORT ZONES

JOSHUA 1:9: "This is my command—be strong and courageous! Do not be afraid or discouraged. For the LORD your God is with you wherever you go."

PSALM 56:3-4: "But when I am afraid, I will put my trust in you. I praise God for what he has promised. I trust in God, so why should I be afraid? What can mere mortals do to me?"

ISAIAH 43:2: "When you go through deep waters, I will be with you. When you go through rivers of difficulty, you will not drown. When you walk through the fire of oppression, you will not be burned up; the flames will not consume you."

PROMISES WHEN WE STEP OUT IN FAITH

PROMISE OF BEING WITH US. DEUTERONOMY 31:6: "So be strong and courageous! Do not be afraid and do not panic before them. For the LORD your God will personally go ahead of you. He will neither fail you nor abandon you."

PROMISE OF NEW THINGS. ISAIAH 43:18-19: "But forget all that—it is nothing compared to what I am going to do. For I am about to do something new. See, I have already begun! Do you not see it? I will make a pathway through the wilderness. I will create rivers in the dry wasteland."

PROMISE OF MIRACLES. MATTHEW 14:29: "'Yes, come,' Jesus said. So, Peter went over the side of the boat and walked on the water toward Jesus."

GRACE TO REBUILD

Think about a spot or routine in your life that feels like a security blanket—something you've been hesitant to step beyond. It could be a physical place or a familiar behavior pattern. Describe this safe place and why it's been your go-to for security.

_____

_____

_____

Consider any moments when fear held you back from diving into the unknown or making a change. Reflect on how the need for predictability played a role in your decisions. Any specific times when you went for predictability instead of potential growth or healing?

_____

_____

_____

Explore the idea of embracing God's guidance and taking a leap beyond your comfort zone with faith. How can you trust God's promise to be with you in the unknown? Any steps you're thinking of taking to conquer fear and move toward the abundant life God has in store for you?

_____

_____

_____

PRAYER

Dear Heavenly Father, as I navigate beyond my comfort zones on this journey, I approach you with an open heart, seeking transformation. Your faithfulness and promises are my anchor, and I'm grateful for them. In this venture, I need your guidance, strength, and presence. Lord, fear often hinders me from stepping into the unknown. Yet, your Word assures me of your constant presence. I find peace in the knowing that you go before me, protecting and guiding me on the right path. Help me lean into your unconditional love courageously and embrace the assurance that you're right beside me. In Jesus's name, I pray. Amen.

EMBRACING THE POSSIBILITIES OF PAIN

Don't copy the behavior and customs of this world, but let
God transform you into a new person by changing the way
you think. Then you will learn to know God's will for you,
which is good and pleasing and perfect. (Romans 12:2)

At times, life's circumstances can push us to our limits. We find ourselves at the end of our strength, raising our hands in surrender and even contemplating giving up. Coming to the end of ourselves could mark the beginning of something beautiful. Surrendering invites the birth of a new version of ourselves—a metamorphosis into the 2.0, new and improved version.

This revised version doesn't merely envision healing but actively takes the essential steps to experience it genuinely. It's a version that welcomes growth and transformation and acknowledges that the old life is gone, and a new life has begun. The new you strives to love others unconditionally, forgive quickly, and recognize the beauty in yourself and others.

The pain we experience can cloud our vision and prevent us from seeing our lives beyond our current challenges. Pain can motivate us to move forward, step back, or stay stuck. Staying paralyzed or moving backward won't position us to discover our God-created purpose or the possibilities of how God might want to use our pain for his purpose. The possibilities of our pain are discovered when we take a step forward, which can be scary. We may face moments of doubt or fear. However, we must take intentional steps forward, focusing on God's restoration promises and relying on his grace, which is his help when we need it most.

If you find yourself at the end of yourself, take heart. It's not the end, but a new beginning. Embrace the possibility of transformation and allow God to birth a new and improved version of you. Surrender your weaknesses, doubts, and fears to him. Trust in his plan and purpose for your life. And remember, God's will for you is good, pleasing, and perfect.

SCRIPTURES ABOUT THE POSSIBILITIES OF PAIN

ROMANS 5:3-5: "We can rejoice, too, when we run into problems and trials, for we know that they help us develop endurance. And endurance develops strength of character, and character strengthens our confident hope of salvation. And this hope will not lead to disappointment. For we know how dearly God loves us, because he has given us the Holy Spirit to fill our hearts with his love."

2 CORINTHIANS 4:17-18: "For our present troubles are small and won't last very long. Yet they produce for us a glory that vastly outweighs them and will last forever! So we don't look at the troubles we can see now; rather, we fix our gaze on things that cannot be seen. For the things we see now will soon be gone, but the things we cannot see will last forever."

JAMES 1:2-4: "Dear brothers and sisters, when troubles of any kind come your way, consider it an opportunity for great joy. For you know that when your faith is tested, your endurance has a chance to grow. So let it grow, for when your endurance is fully developed, you will be perfect and complete, needing nothing."

PROMISES FOR OUR PAIN

PROMISE OF DANCING. PSALM 30:11-12: "You have turned my mourning into joyful dancing. You have taken away my clothes of mourning and clothed me with joy, that I might sing praises to you and not be silent. O LORD my God, I will give you thanks forever!"

PROMISE OF FRESH BEGINNINGS. ISAIAH 43:18-19: "But forget all that—it is nothing compared to what I am going to do. For I am about to do something new. See, I have already begun! Do you not see it? I will make a pathway through the wilderness. I will create rivers in the dry wasteland."

PROMISE OF GOOD THINGS. ROMANS 8:28: "And we know that God causes everything to work together for the good of those who love God and are called according to his purpose for them."

GRACE TO REBUILD

Take a moment to reflect on your divorce, separation, or any tough season you've been through. Describe the emotions, doubts, or fears you encountered. How did this pain affect your perspective and actions?

_____

_____

_____

Think about stepping into a "2.0" version of yourself. What changes or growth are you seeing as you move on from those tough times? How is God's healing and transformational power showing up in your life?

_____

_____

_____

Ponder on God's restoration promises. How can you weave these promises into your journey through pain and transformation? What steps might you take to trust in God's plan, release your weaknesses, and embrace the possibilities for healing and growth?

_____

_____

_____

PRAYER

Dear Heavenly Father, thank you for the opportunity of transformation and growth. I surrender my old ways and open myself to the work of the Holy Spirit. Renew my mind and align my thoughts with your truth. Help me to love unconditionally, forgive quickly, and embrace the beauty in myself and others. Strengthen me to take the necessary steps toward healing and wholeness. I trust your promises to complete the 2.0 transformation you have already started in me. In Jesus's name, I pray. Amen.

I NEED AN UPGRADE

*I will exchange your bronze for gold, your iron for silver, your
wood for bronze, and your stones for iron. I will make peace
your leader and righteousness your ruler. (Isaiah 60:17)*

There comes a time when we must decide to move forward. My counselor told me I was being held back by fear.

"Fear?" I said. "Me? That couldn't be. I'm not afraid of anything."

My counselor shook her head. "Tracy, you're afraid of stepping through the doors God is opening for you. But you can do it, if you acknowledge your fear and hand that fear over to the Lord."

I listened to her, prayed, closed my eyes, gritted my teeth, and decided to trust God to upgrade me with what I needed to make the next move. So, I had a conversation with God about my desire for an upgrade. Here is my journal entry of my talk with him:

*God, I desire an upgrade. I need to move from where I
am to where you have destined me to be. I must climb to
a new height to reach my calling, but I'm afraid the next
step is a big one. I require your power to help me conquer
fear and your strength to push beyond my comfort zone.*

*Can we do an exchange? I will surrender my fear of failure
in exchange for your assistance. I need confidence and
passion to propel me ahead. What is keeping me stagnant is
insignificant compared to the possibilities awaiting. My next-
level potential far outweighs the comfort of staying safe.*

*Today I decided to trust you, knowing you are with me.
I will not allow my mind to continue to deceive me
into thinking advancing is insurmountable. Instead,
I will take the risk and step into my new place.*

*I did it—I'm at the next level, propelled by your strength
and guidance. Today marks the beginning of my journey
toward my purpose. I refuse to look back. The past is no
longer comfortable when my full potential awaits. I am
ready to embrace the challenges, the growth, and the victories
that come with pursuing your calling for my life.*

*Thank you for being my inspiration. With you by
my side, I am confident I can do the impossible and
overcome any fear. Empower, guide, and help me
walk confidently, knowing I am called to by you.*

It's time for you to take a stand against any opposition keeping you
stagnant from fully walking into your upgrade season.

SCRIPTURES ABOUT GOD'S UPGRADE

EZEKIEL 36:26-27: "And I will give you a new heart, and I will put a new spirit in you. I will take out your stony, stubborn heart and give you a tender, responsive heart. And I will put my Spirit in you so that you will follow my decrees and be careful to obey my regulations."

GALATIANS 5:22-23: "But the Holy Spirit produces this kind of fruit in our lives: love, joy, peace, patience, kindness, goodness, faithfulness, gentleness, and self-control. There is no law against these things!"

EPHESIANS 4:22-24: "Throw off your old sinful nature and your former way of life, which is corrupted by lust and deception. Instead, let the Spirit renew your thoughts and attitudes. Put on your new nature, created to be like God—truly righteous and holy."

GOD'S RESTORATION PROMISE TO UPGRADE

PROMISE TO HONOR. PSALM 23:3: "He renews my strength. He guides me along right paths, bringing honor to his name."

PROMISE TO SOAR OVER CIRCUMSTANCES. ISAIAH 40:31: "But those who trust in the LORD will find new strength. They will soar high on wings like eagles. They will run and not grow weary. They will walk and not faint."

PROMISE OF EVERYTHING NEW. REVELATION 21:5: "And the one sitting on the throne said, 'Look, I am making everything new!' And then he said to me, 'Write this down, for what I tell you is trustworthy and true.'"

GRACE TO REBUILD

Take a moment to think about the fears or hesitations holding you back from moving forward. What are they, and how have they influenced your decisions and actions?

_____

_____

_____

Picture having a heart-to-heart with God. What areas of your life are you hoping for an upgrade in? Write a letter or a journal entry talking to God about your desires, fears, and willingness to trust him for an upgrade.

_____

_____

_____

Imagine you have conquered your fears and embraced the upgrade God has for you. Describe this future version of yourself and the possibilities in front of you. What steps can you take today to start walking toward this upgraded version of your life?

_____

_____

_____

PRAYER

Dear Heavenly Father, I recognize fear is holding me back, inhibiting me from stepping into the opportunities you offer. I choose to surrender my fear in exchange for your strength and confidence. Empower me to move from where I am to where you've destined me to be. With your guidance, I'm ready to take the leap, embracing the upgrade you have for me. Thank you for being my inspiration, and I trust in power to help me leap farther than I have before.

In Jesus's name, I pray. Amen.

PART 3

HOPE IN GOD'S PROMISES

God is not a man, so he does not lie. He is not human, so he does not change his mind. Has he ever spoken and failed to act? Has he ever promised and not carried it through? (Numbers 23:19)

ARISE AND POSSESS: CLAIMING YOUR INHERITANCE

So be strong and courageous! Do not be afraid and do not panic before them. For the LORD your God will personally go ahead of you. He will neither fail you nor abandon you. (Deuteronomy 31:6)

The book of Joshua narrates God's guidance of his people into Canaan, their promised land inheritance. Canaan represented prosperity and a fresh start. Joshua was appointed as the leader for this assignment. I'm sure he experienced a mixture of excitement and trepidation as he embarked on leading the Israelites. In Joshua 1:2-9, to encourage and empower him, God provided Joshua with seven instructions and promises:

1. "Therefore, the time has come for you to lead these people, the Israelites, across the Jordan River into the land I am giving them."

2. "Wherever you set foot, you will be on land I have given you—from the Negev wilderness in the south to the Lebanon mountains in the north, from the Euphrates River in the east of the Mediterranean Sea in the West, including all the land of the Hittites."

3. "No one will be able to stand against you as long as you live. For I will be with you as I was with Moses. I will not fail you or abandon you."

4. "Be strong and courageous, for you are the one who will lead these people to possess all the land I swore to their ancestors I would give them."

5. "Be strong and very courageous. Be careful to obey all the instructions Moses gave you. Do not deviate from them, turning either to the right or to the left. Then you will be successful in all you do."

6. "Study this Book of Instruction continually. Meditate on it day and night so you will be sure to obey everything written in it. Only then will you prosper and succeed in all you do."

7. "This is my command—be strong and courageous! Do not be afraid or discouraged. For the Lord your God is with you wherever you go."

Are you transitioning from a wilderness season and need guidance to move into a new territory? God knows stepping into unknown territory is scary, especially when we face challenging situations and can't see what is ahead of us. Just as he encouraged Joshua by promising him strength and courage three times, he also wants to remind us that our challenges don't detract from what we're destined to receive. Our promised inheritance is still within reach.

Be encouraged. When God calls us for an assignment, he equips us with the power to fulfill it. There is no reason to fear because he is beside us wherever we go. The promises he gave Joshua are our promises too.

While we move forward boldly and courageously, obeying God's Word and meditating on it day and night, success will follow us.

SCRIPTURES ABOUT GOD'S PROMISED INHERITANCE

EPHESIANS 1:11: "Furthermore, because we are united with Christ, we have received an inheritance from God, for he chose us in advance, and he makes everything work out according to his plan."

PHILIPPIANS 1:6: "And I am certain that God, who began the good work within you, will continue his work until it is finally finished on the day when Christ Jesus returns."

ROMANS 15:13: "I pray that God, the source of hope, will fill you completely with joy and peace because you trust in him. Then you will overflow with confident hope through the power of the Holy Spirit."

GOD'S PROMISES FOR OUR INHERITANCE

PROMISE TO RESTORE LOSS. JOEL 2:25-26: "The LORD says, 'I will give you back what you lost to the swarming locusts, the hopping locusts, the stripping locusts, and the cutting locusts. It was I who sent this great destroying army against you. Once again you will have all the food you want, and you will praise the LORD your God, who does these miracles for you. Never again will my people be disgraced.'"

PROMISE TO REMOVE SHAME. ISAIAH 61:7: "Instead of shame and dishonor, you will enjoy a double share of honor. You will possess a double portion of prosperity in your land, and everlasting joy will be yours."

PROMISE TO BE OUR GUARD. PSALM 16:5-6: "LORD, you alone are my inheritance, my cup of blessing. You guard all that is mine. The land you have given me is a pleasant land. What a wonderful inheritance!"

GRACE TO REBUILD

After dealing with a divorce or separation, what parts of yourself or your life feel like they've taken a hit? Take a moment to reflect on how these losses have affected you. How can you start picking up the pieces and bring back those important parts of who you are? Any ideas on how to kickstart your healing journey?

_____

_____

_____

Thinking about God's promise to be strong and courageous, how does that show up in your life? Remember those moments when your faith gave you a boost during tough times? How can you keep relying on that promise while you're navigating through all the changes and uncertainties?

_____

_____

_____

Do you have any goals or plans for this new chapter you're navigating—in in your personal life, relationships, or anywhere else? Take some time to figure out what you're aiming for and picture the awesome future you want. What practical steps can you take to make those dreams a reality?

_____

_____

_____

PRAYER

Dear Heavenly Father, I am grateful for the story of Joshua and the promises you gave him during his leadership of the Israelites into the Promised Land. As you equipped and uplifted Joshua, I ask for your guidance, strength, and encouragement. Strengthen me for the journey ahead. I can't see what is on the other side, but I want to release my uncertainties and embrace your promises. Instill fresh hope, joy, and peace within me as I trust you. In Jesus's name, I pray. Amen.

RENEWED BEAUTY

*Don't be concerned about the outward beauty of
fancy hairstyles, expensive jewelry, or beautiful
clothes. You should clothe yourselves instead
with the beauty that comes from within, the
unfading beauty of a gentle and quiet spirit,
which is so precious to God. (1 Peter 3:3 -4)*

After being divorced for two years, I considered returning to the dating scene. But when I looked at my reflection in the mirror, I had aged.

The divorce process impacted my appearance and self-esteem, causing me to struggle with recognizing my own worth due to feeling unattractive. This left me questioning whether others could perceive my beauty. Probably not. Feeling discouraged, I decided to postpone my dating aspirations. Instead, I focused on rebuilding my chaotic life by caring for my spiritual, emotional, and physical well-being.

Psalm 103:5 reminds us that "He fills my life with good things. My youth is renewed like the eagle's!" Connecting with God is the ultimate makeover. Over time, he replaced my worries and tired countenance with peace, a radiant smile, and the enthusiasm and vigor of my youth. This inner satisfaction started to reflect in my appearance. Others often said, "You're radiant—what beauty products do you use?"

I'd smile and respond by mentioning I use the "peace" skincare line. I understood that investing in meaningful moments with God is the ultimate approach to refreshing my inner self and outward appearance. We can spend significant moments with God by setting aside a portion of our day to talk with him, invite him into our thoughts, and prioritize him as the center of our attention.

In moments spent with God, he offers us a fresh outlook and resilience to live without being burdened by stress, anxiety, depression, or fear—all the things depleting us. Investing time in our relationship with God yields remarkable rewards. Our inner strength flourishes, enabling us to transition from feeling finished to being refreshed.

Consider letting go of anything draining you. Instead, look for things that replenish your spirit. Take back your peacetime. Re-direct your focus. Make new memories. Meet new friends or anything else to help you flow into the extraordinary callings God blessed you with to advance his kingdom. Enroll in a class, try a new hobby, volunteer time, read your Bible, and attend a supportive church.

Others are drawn to our external beauty because we bring the scent of Christ, a beautiful fragrance, beyond our reflection. Our value is remarkable because God is a master carpenter. His work is flawless— he transforms everything into beautiful at the right moment.

SCRIPTURES ABOUT
HOW GOD SEES HIS DAUGHTERS

SONG OF SOLOMON 4:7: "You are altogether beautiful, my darling, beautiful in every way."

PROVERBS 31:25-26: "She is clothed with strength and dignity, and she laughs without fear of the future. When she speaks, her words are wise, and she gives instructions with kindness."

EPHESIANS 2:10 "For we are God's masterpiece. He has created us anew in Christ Jesus, so we can do the good things he planned for us long ago."

GOD'S PROMISES FOR PEACE AND JOY

PROMISE OF CONFIDENT HOPE. ROMANS 15:13: "I pray that God, the source of hope, will fill you completely with joy and peace because you trust in him. Then you will overflow with confident hope through the power of the Holy Spirit."

PROMISE OF PEACE OF MIND. JOHN 14:27: "I am leaving you with a gift—peace of mind and heart. And the peace I give is a gift the world cannot give. So don't be troubled or afraid."

PROMISE OF A GOOD FUTURE. JEREMIAH 29:11: "For I know the plans I have for you," says the LORD. "They are plans for good and not for disaster, to give you a future and a hope."

GRACE TO REBUILD

Reflecting on your journey after separation or divorce, what emotions arise when you think about your self-esteem and appearance? How has this experience shaped your perception of your worth and attractiveness?

_____

_____

_____

Consider a time when you've felt the refreshing presence of God, experiencing renewed strength and peace. How did this inner transformation manifest outwardly? How might embracing the "peace" skincare line as a metaphor for God's renewal encourages you?

_____

_____

_____

Looking at your present life, are there areas where you feel depleted or drained? What practical steps can you take to prioritize spending quality time with God and investing in your well-being? How might this investment impact both your inner self and your outward appearance?

_____

_____

_____

PRAYER

Dear Heavenly Father, I thank you for the healing power of your presence. I seek strength and renewal as I connect with you, embracing your promise of transformation and peace. Through intentional moments with you, I can find protection against stress and anxiety, gain inner strength, and transition from depletion to renewal. I desire to prioritize your presence and release what burdens me. I trust your promise to create beauty from my ashes. Your view of my worth gives me strength, dignity, and wisdom. I claim your promise of restoration and find peace and joy in your good plans as I step into the future. In Jesus's name, I pray. Amen.

DO YOU NEED PROTECTION?

For he will rescue you from every trap and protect
you from deadly disease. (Psalm 91:3)

Psalm 91 shows how God is a protector. It's reassuring to know he is our security guard, along with his angels. This psalm tells us if we trust him instead of relying on other things, he will save us and keep us safe from the traps set by the enemy.

The enemy's goal is to stop us. He wants to divert our attention from our identity in Christ and from the strength we have when we trust God. Psalm 91 sets up an "if and then" proposition, signifying specific actions on our part lead to corresponding responses from God.

Here are a few instances:

"When you abide under the shadow of Shaddai, you are hidden in the strength of God Most High." Psalm 91:1 (TPT)

"When we live our lives within the shadow of God Most High, our secret hiding place, we will always be shielded from harm." Psalm 91:9-10 (TPT)

"Because you have loved me, delighted in me, and have been loyal to my name, I will greatly protect you." Psalm 91:14 (TPT)

"I will answer your cry for help every time you pray, and you will feel my presence in the time of trouble. I will deliver you and bring you honor." Psalm 91:15 (TPT)

"I will satisfy you with a full life and with all that I do for you. You will enjoy the fullness of my salvation." Psalm 91:16 (TPT)

The consistent message conveyed in Psalm 91 is that when we rely on God, he will place us under his care and protect us despite our challenging and difficult times. When evil comes our way, it won't destroy or hurt us because we have made God our habitation.

A habitation is where we live or where we call home. It's not a place we visit occasionally, but our consistent resting place. How do we make God our habitation?

1. Not depending on our jobs, homes, families, or anything else as the primary source for our security.

2. Practicing being in God's presence every day.

3. Focusing our thoughts, actions, and desires on his ways, not ours.

4. Praising and worshiping him and consistently receiving instructions from our life's handbook—the Bible.

Psalm 91 reminds us that God is our ultimate protector and refuge. We find a shield against harm and deliverance from the enemy's snares as we place our trust in him and dwell in his presence. By making God our habitation and consistently relying on his strength, we walk forward with the assurance that his wings are our secure covering. God's presence protects us completely, so run home and let God cover you.

SCRIPTURES ABOUT GOD'S PROTECTION

PSALM 91:1-2: "Those who live in the shelter of the Most High will find rest in the shadow of the Almighty. This I declare about the LORD: He alone is my refuge, my place of safety; he is my God, and I trust him."

PSALM 91:4: "He will cover you with his feathers. He will shelter you with his wings. His faithful promises are your armor and protection."

PSALM 91:7: "Though a thousand fall at your side, though ten thousand are dying around you, these evils will not touch you."

PROMISES TO KEEP US SAFE

PROMISE OF ANGELIC PROTECTION 24/7. PSALM 91:11: "For he will order his angels to protect you wherever you go."

PROMISE TO RESCUE. PSALM 91:15: "When they call on me, I will answer; I will be with them in trouble. I will rescue and honor them."

PROMISE OF SHELTER FROM EVIL. PSALM 91:9-10: "If you make the LORD your refuge, if you make the Most High your shelter, no evil will conquer you; no plague will come near your home."

GRACE TO REBUILD

Have you ever found yourself in a vulnerable situation where you needed protection? How did you manage it? Did you turn to God as your ultimate source of protection, or did you seek security elsewhere?

_____

_____

_____

What do you think about making God your constant refuge, like a "home base"? How can you adjust your focus to rely more on God's presence and guidance in your daily life?

_____

_____

_____

Consider Psalm 91 and its "if and then" structure. Could you adopt any specific behaviors or mindsets to activate God's promised protection? How can you intentionally position yourself under the shelter of the Most High and feel the Almighty's presence around you?

_____

_____

_____

PRAYER

Dear Heavenly Father, in Psalm 91, I see your promises to protect me. Help me rely on you, not on temporary things. I desire your presence to be my constant habitation. Please guide me to align my thoughts, actions, and desires with your ways. I'm grateful for the shield your presence provides and your assurance that you cover me with your feathers, shield me with your wings, and guard me from harm. I'm reassured knowing I am completely protected, and you promise to answer me in times of trouble. In Jesus's name, I pray. Amen.

JUST BE FREE!

We escaped like a bird from a hunter's trap. The trap is broken, and we are free! Our help is from the LORD, who made heaven and earth. (Psalm 124:7-8)

Have you ever said to yourself, "I want to be free?" After my divorce, a friend told me I must live in the moment. I pursed my lips. What does live in the moment mean?

I researched the phrase, and it means to let all else go, not move back in time, be present in thought, and not jump ahead to the future. Living in the moment also requires us to escape from mindsets that keep us trapped: doing things the same way, overanalyzing situations, and manipulating others.

To live in the moment, we must be flexible, patient, and willing to change our thoughts and emotional responses toward uncomfortable and uncontrollable situations. Staying offended, controlling everything, and being fearful are all mindsets preventing us from living in the moment. Living in the moment is challenging because it requires us to trust God and more than ourselves.

While I processed the definition of living in the moment, I realized I didn't know how to do that. My friend's observation of me was correct. My automatic default is to analyze, fix, solve, daydream, and ponder the past. Because I love challenges, I decided to work toward living in the moment as one of my goals.

Some live-in-the-moment dos and don'ts:

1. Do understand the value of our time. Stop spending days, weeks, and months worrying about what might happen. Rehearsing the different worst-case scenarios in our heads is a waste of time.

2. Do be okay with having only some of the answers. Saying we don't know and letting someone else figure it out is fine.

3. Don't jump ahead of God by deciding what is best. Stop establishing timelines for him when we want something to happen. Waiting on God's timing will help us avoid getting confused and upset when our expectations don't become a reality.

4. Don't pull away from today. Spending our day focused on issues we can't resolve, such as a bill due next month or any other consuming thought, wastes time.

God has solutions and blessings for us in our here and now. Whether good, bad, or indifferent, we don't have to plan or process our problems away. If we keep projecting ourselves into the future, we might miss out on what God wants to show us today.

SCRIPTURES ABOUT LIVING FREE

MATTHEW 6:34: "So don't worry about tomorrow, for tomorrow will bring its own worries. Today's trouble is enough for today."

ECCLESIASTES 3:1, 6: "For everything there is a season, a time for every activity under heaven. A time to search and a time to quit searching. A time to keep and a time to throw away."

JAMES 4:13-14: "Look here, you who say, 'Today or tomorrow we are going to a certain town and will stay there a year. We will do business there and make a profit.' How do you know what your life will be like tomorrow? Your life is like the morning fog—it's here a little while, then it's gone."

PROMISES WHEN WE LIVE IN THE MOMENT

PROMISE OF PEACE. PHILIPPIANS 4:6-7: "Don't worry about anything; instead, pray about everything. Tell God what you need and thank him for all he has done. Then you will experience God's peace, which exceeds anything we can understand. His peace will guard your hearts and minds as you live in Christ Jesus."

PROMISE OF ORDERED STEPS. PROVERBS 16:9: "We can make our plans, but the LORD determines our steps."

PROMISE OF PROVISIONS. MATTHEW 6:25-26: "That is why I tell you not to worry about everyday life—whether you have enough food and drink, or enough clothes to wear. Isn't life more than food, and your body more than clothing? Look at the birds. They don't plant or harvest or store food in barns, for your heavenly Father feeds them. And aren't you far more valuable to him than they are?"

GRACE TO REBUILD

Reflect on a recent situation in which you focused on the past or worried excessively about the future. How did this mindset affect your emotions and overall well-being?

_____

_____

_____

Consider a moment when you were fully engaged in the present. How did that feel? What were the circumstances that allowed you to maintain focus on the present?

_____

_____

_____

Review the ""live-in-the-moment do's and don'ts." Which of these resonates with you the most, and why? Are there any specific steps you can take to implement these principles in your daily life and break free from any patterns that hinder living in the moment?

_____

_____

_____

PRAYER

Dear Heavenly Father, I seek the freedom to live in the moment. Just as a bird escapes a trap, I want to be free from overthinking and worrying. Teach me to trust your guidance and release my need to control outcomes. Please help me find contentment each day, seeking your peace that surpasses all understanding. Please grant me the wisdom to let go of the past and trust your perfect timing. As I strive to live freely in the present, I want to experience your presence and blessings. In Jesus's name, I pray. Amen.

GOD'S FUNNY GIRL

He will once again fill your mouth with laughter
and your lips with shouts of joy. (Job 8:21)

Can you remember the last time you laughed so hard that you gave yourself an ab workout? In my younger days, my family often remarked about my comical personality. The realities of life—responsibilities, deadlines, and letdowns—caused my funny girl to fade into the background. The get-it-done girl emerged. She sneaked in as an uninvited guest and convinced me to stop laughing.

As life progresses, our daily routines can become hurried, stressful, and robotic. We can organize our day to the minute and make time for God, family, and our ministries. But can we still schedule time for ourselves. We need to find ways to refill to avoid operating from a place of depletion, expressing the creative gifts that make us unique and beautiful. It's challenging to be everything to everybody while still caring for our well-being and permitting ourselves to laugh until it hurts sometimes. Achieving this balance has led to a new awareness in myself.

God showed me the significance of laughter. I now recognize being silly as one of my superpowers. He made me a funny girl. Laughing is something I must do every day because my good humor puts the Jesus in me on display.

The enemy continues to try to silence my laughter to steal my witness. If my disposition displays anger or sadness instead of joy, my calling will not effectively point others to Jesus as their deliverer. God gave us the gift of laughter for the following reasons:

୧ To heal us, reduce stress, and lower blood pressure. In Proverbs 17:22, King Solomon, the wisest man who ever lived, said, "A cheerful heart is a good medicine, but a broken spirit saps a person's strength."

୧ To express our inward excitement for the Lord. In Psalm 126:2–3, King David reminds us, "We were filled with laughter, and we sang for joy. And the other nations said, "What amazing things the LORD has done for them." Our laughter conveys God's greatness in our lives.

୧ To strengthen our connection with others. Most people enjoy being around humorous people. Laughter is contagious and can also be an effective witnessing tool.

God desires for the fun side within us to shine bright, revealing our freedom, creativity, and the beauty of our smile, which radiates hope and peace to those around us. Ask him to reveal the funny girl in you and how your laughter can become a powerful witnessing tool to reflect the presence of Jesus in your life.

SCRIPTURES ABOUT LAUGHTER

LUKE 6:21: "God blesses you who are hungry now, for you will be satisfied. God blesses you who weep now, for in due time you will laugh."

PROVERBS 31:25: "She is clothed with strength and dignity, and she laughs without fear of the future."

PSALM 30:11: "You have turned my mourning into joyful dancing. You have taken away my clothes of mourning and clothed me with joy."

PROMISES ABOUT LAUGHTER

PROMISE TO PROTECT OUR EMOTIONAL HEART. PROVERBS 14:13: "Laughter can conceal a heavy heart, but when the laughter ends, the grief remains."

PROMISE OF TIMES OF LAUGHTER. ECCLESIASTES 3:4: "A time to cry and a time to laugh. A time to grieve and a time to dance."

PROMISE OF JOY. JEREMIAH 31:13: "The young women will dance for joy, and the men—old and young—will join in the celebration. I will turn their mourning into joy. I will comfort them and exchange their sorrow for rejoicing."

GRACE TO REBUILD

Reflect on a recent moment when you laughed. How did it bring a sense of lightness to your day? Consider the last time you embraced your funny girl persona and its impact on your mood and interactions.

_____

_____

_____

Examine your daily routine and commitments. Are you prioritizing time for yourself and your well-being, including moments of cheer and laughter? How can you schedule moments of laughter and self-care amidst your responsibilities and obligations as you navigate the challenges of divorce or separation?

_____

_____

_____

Consider the significance of laughter as a gift from God in times of difficulty and transition. How does laughing contribute to your overall well-being? How might your laughter serve to express your joy from the Lord and connect with others on a deeper level?

_____

_____

_____

PRAYER

Dear Heavenly Father, I embrace the gift of laughter as a source of joy and healing. In life's busyness, help me rediscover my "funny girl" spirit. Let my laughter testify to your love as you help me overcome challenges. Guard me against joy robbers and restore my ability to find humor even in difficulties. May my laughter uplift others and reflect your joy. Thank you for the gift of laughter and the freedom it brings. In Jesus's name. Amen.

PART 4

HOPE IN GOD'S LAVISHING LOVE

See how very much our Father loves us, for he calls us his children, and that is what we are! But the people who belong to this world don't recognize that we are God's children because they don't know him. (1 John 3:1)

EMBRACING GOD'S LOVE DURING STRUGGLES

*In his kindness God called you to share in his
eternal glory by means of Christ Jesus. So after
you have suffered a little while, he will restore,
support, and strengthen you, and he will place
you on a firm foundation. (1 Peter 5:10)*

While healing from my divorce, I contemplated overcoming my difficulties, curious about when relief from the pain would come and what shape my new normal would take. Despite my uncertainty about this upcoming phase, I believed that God's vision for my life would outshine my present struggles, and hope would eventually dissolve all traces of disappointment.

Sometimes, the first reaction to experiencing the deep disappointment of a broken relationship is to withdraw and isolate. During emotional struggles, the best thing we can do is reach out to a friend, loved one, or counselor and become vulnerable about our feelings despite the shame we might experience.

When my divorce journey began, I wasted no time seeking help through counseling. The pain in my stomach and the overwhelming fear in my thoughts pushed me to find answers. I met an incredible woman, a biblical prayer counselor, who not only became my mentor and prayer companion but also shared with me the profound truth of God's unconditional love and his power to mend and renew my spirit.

One day, while I cried in one of my sessions, my counselor told me pain is God's gift to us. With a perplexed look, I asked, "How is pain a gift?" She explained pain signifies something is off track.

Pain is God's way of getting our attention, saving us from ourselves, and healing us. Her explanation about the power of afflictions shifted my perspective on this significant transition in my life. Instead of chasing my pain, I began to chase getting healed by submitting myself to God. True freedom comes from being vulnerable and not being sufficient in ourselves but embracing the hope, peace, and love only God can provide.

When life gets tough, and the weight of the world is on our shoulders, God's loving kindness rescues us at the right time. First Peter 5:10 reminds us that after we've endured our fair share of pain, God steps in to heal our hearts, lift us when we're at our lowest, and give us new strength. He becomes the solid rock keeping us steady during our darkest moments, offering a helping hand to pull us through turbulent times. God's help is his tangible love on display.

While you struggle with emotional pain, I encourage you to reach out to God and seek his guidance and peace. Don't hesitate to lean on a friend or family member who can support you as a trusted advisor or a prayer companion. Let God and your loved ones surround you with love and care.

SCRIPTURES ABOUT EMBRACING
GOD'S PROMISE DURING OUR STRUGGLES

ISAIAH 41:10: "Don't be afraid, for I am with you. Don't be discouraged, for I am your God. I will strengthen you and help you. I will hold you up with my victorious right hand."

PSALM 34:17-18: "The LORD hears his people when they call to him for help. He rescues them from all their troubles. The LORD is close to the brokenhearted; he rescues those whose spirits are crushed."

2 CORINTHIANS 1:4: "He comforts us in all our troubles so that we can comfort others. When they are troubled, we will be able to give them the same comfort God has given us."

PROMISES DURING OUR STRUGGLES

PROMISE OF GOD'S HELP. PSALM 46:1: "God is our refuge and strength, always ready to help in times of trouble."

PROMISE OF GOD LIFTING BURDENS. MATTHEW 11:28-30: "Then Jesus said, 'Come to me, all of you who are weary and carry heavy burdens, and I will give you rest. Take my yoke upon you. Let me teach you because I am humble and gentle at heart, and you will find rest for your souls. For my yoke is easy to bear, and the burden I give you is light.'"

PROMISE OF NOT FALLING. PSALM 55:22: "Give your burdens to the LORD, and he will take care of you. He will not permit the godly to slip and fall."

GRACE TO REBUILD

Pain can sometimes be a signpost telling us something might not be going right in our lives. God uses tough moments to nudge us toward growth and healing. How do you see this idea when you're dealing with the ups and downs of divorce or separation?

_____

_____

_____

What do you think about the idea of pain being a gift? How do you think this viewpoint could shape how you approach healing and your faith in God during this time?

_____

_____

_____

Who are the people who've been there for you during this whole process? How do you think you can lean on them more? Maybe as advisors, confidants, or even prayer buddies as you navigate through this chapter of your life?

_____

_____

_____

PRAYER

Dear Heavenly Father, thank you for being my constant source of kindness and love throughout the ups and downs of life. As I look back on my path of pain and healing, your love has truly touched me. There were times when I doubted if the pain would ever ease up. But having the people you've brought into my life has been such a blessing. Their love showed me the extent of your unconditional love and ability to heal. Whenever things got tough, it was your loving kindness that pulled me through. Lord, today I pray for myself and anyone going through emotional struggles. May we find the courage to reach out to you for guidance and peace, and may we have the support of loved ones who can provide comfort. In Jesus's name, I pray. Amen.

KISSED BY GOD

Jesus looked at them intently and said, "Humanly speaking, it is impossible. But with God everything is possible." (Matthew 19:26)

Thinking about your next moves involves considering the goals and dreams you desire to achieve, the places you wish to visit, and your strategies for making them a reality. Many exciting adventures lie ahead. However, the more significant consideration is whether you've sought God's approval for your ideas.

At one point, while I considered my aspirations for the upcoming year, I turned to prayer. To my surprise, God's response was clear: "I want you to begin writing a weekly devotional." I couldn't help but chuckle at his directive. Writing had never been one of my talents, and English was not a subject I enjoyed in school.

While I considered fulfilling God's request, he reassured me, "If you follow my guidance and obey, I will inspire your writing, not in advance but each week. I will also bring healing to both you and others through your words."

God had my attention, so I got motivated and started an unfamiliar journey of sending out a weekly devotional blog. Each week, God inspired me on what to write. There were moments when I read my words and thought, "Did I write this?" My writing did indeed bring healing to my wounded heart and helped others.

Today, I am a published author. The journey to that title was something I never thought possible. During the darkest days of my divorce, if someone had told me God would take my pain and turn it into a ministry and evangelism tool, I would have laughed in disbelief. Not in a million years. I'm no writer.

Accomplishing anything sustainable or beneficial to us, others, and God must be kissed—approved by God. Our goals will be challenging to achieve. Roadblocks will occur, and our plans will eventually dissolve if God is not involved.

Our goal might be exciting, but is it God's idea? God can take our goals and dreams much farther than we can imagine. The Holy Spirit helps to move us past the things blocking our movement forward. The Holy Spirit is our best supporter, giving us the strategy and going ahead of us to help accomplish our plans.

God loves for you to dream. Consider how he might want to use your current circumstances to heal you or minister to others. Ensure your aspirations align with God's plan. Make sure your why is rooted in the things God wants to accomplish. The impossible becomes possible when your goals are God's.

SCRIPTURES ABOUT
GOD SUPPORTING OUR PLANS

PROVERBS 20:24: "The LORD directs our steps, so why try to understand everything along the way?"

PROVERBS 19:21: "You can make many plans, but the LORD's purpose will prevail."

JAMES 4:13-15: "Look here, you who say, 'Today or tomorrow we are going to a certain town and will stay there a year. We will do business there and make a profit. How do you know what your life will be like tomorrow? Your life is like the morning fog—it's here a little while, then it's gone. What you ought to say is, 'If the Lord wants us to, we will live and do this or that.'"

PROMISES WHEN WE ALIGN OUR PLANS
WITH GOD'S PLANS

PROMISE OF HIS HELP. PSALM 37:4-5: "Take delight in the LORD, and he will give you your heart's desires. Commit everything you do to the LORD. Trust him, and he will help you."

PROMISE OF HEARING HIS VOICE. ISAIAH 30:21: "Your own ears will hear him. Right behind you, a voice will say, 'This is the way you should go,' whether to the right or to the left."

PROMISE OF PLANS SUCCEEDING. PROVERBS 16:3: "Commit your actions to the LORD, and your plans will succeed."

GRACE TO REBUILD

Reflect on your current goals and dreams. Are you considering God's approval and guidance in your plans? Why or why not?

_____

_____

_____

Have you ever received a surprising directive or calling from God? How did you initially react, and how did you eventually respond?

_____

_____

_____

Have you experienced situations in which your goals aligned with God's plan, and you witnessed the impossible becoming possible? Describe those experiences.

_____

_____

_____

PRAYER

Dear Heavenly Father, I seek your guidance and wisdom as I pursue my goals and dreams. I don't want to miss what you are asking me to do. Please reveal your plans for my life. Help me align my aspirations with your will. I trust in your promise of success when I commit my actions to you. Holy Spirit, empower me, remove obstacles, and lead me forward. I thank you for your constant support and pray for the impossible becoming possible as I pursue your direction and plans for me. In Jesus's name, I pray. Amen.

DELIGHTING IN GOD: THE KEY TO YOUR HEART'S DESIRES

Take delight in the LORD, and he will give you your heart's desires.
(Psalm 37:4)

The Christmas season is my favorite time of the year. That's when I start to think about leaving the old and embracing the new. One day, while shopping, I became intrigued by a framed picture with the inscription: "Something wonderful is about to happen."

Of course, I purchased it because it described my expectations from God. That particular year, I sensed a different type of hope and expectation. Something amazing will evolve soon. Would he answer a prayer or open a door of opportunity? Would I finally get to the other side of my divorce?

Our only option is often to wait on God's timing to bring our heart's desires or prayers to fruition. In Psalm 37:4, David tells us we are supposed to delight ourselves or take joy in our relationship with God; if we do, he will give us the things we desire. Delighting in someone means we enjoy being with them and want to please them.

In Psalm 27:4, David is seeking after one thing, what he desired most—to live with God every moment, delighting in his glory and grace. David craved God's presence. Intimacy with his Father fulfilled the desires of his heart.

We also have a few ways we can delight ourselves in the Lord:

    ☙ Doing God's Will. "I take joy in doing your will, my God, for your instructions are written on my heart." (Psalm 40:8)

    ☙ Being Honest. "The LORD detests lying lips, but he delights in those who tell the truth." (Proverbs 12:22)

    ☙ Obeying God. "But Samuel replied, 'What is more pleasing to the LORD: Your burnt offerings and sacrifices or your obedience to his voice? Listen! Obedience is better than sacrifice, and submission is better than offering the fat of rams.'" (1 Samuel 15:22)

    ☙ Praying. "The LORD detests the sacrifice of the wicked, but he delights in the prayers of the upright." (Proverbs 15:8)

    ☙ Living a Righteous Life. "Make me walk along the path of your commands, for that is where my happiness is found." (Psalm 119:35)

Do you desire peace, restoration, or healing? God promises us if we desire him first, he will give us our desires.

SCRIPTURES ABOUT DESIRING GOD

PSALM 42:1-2: "As the deer longs for streams of water, so I long for you, O God. I thirst for God, the living God. When can I go and stand before him?"

PSALM 73:25-26: "Whom have I in heaven but you? I desire you more than anything on earth. My health may fail, and my spirit may grow weak, but God remains the strength of my heart; he is mine forever."

PSALM 119:131: "I pant with expectation, longing for your commands."

PROMISES WHEN WE DESIRE GOD

PROMISE OF NEEDS MEET. MATTHEW 6:33: "Seek the Kingdom of God above all else, and live righteously, and he will give you everything you need."

PROMISE OF FINDING HIM. JEREMIAH 29:13: "If you look for me wholeheartedly, you will find me."

PROMISE OF RECEIVING HIS LOVE, COMPASSION, AND HELP. ISAIAH 30:18: "So the LORD must wait for you to come to him so he can show you his love and compassion. For the LORD is a faithful God. Blessed are those who wait for his help."

GRACE TO REBUILD

Take some time to consider your heart's desires. What are the things that truly matter to you—the things you long for deep down? How do these desires align with your relationship with God, and how might delighting in him impact these desires?

_____

_____

_____

Psalm 27:4 mentions David's desire to spend time in God's presence and fall more in love with him. How can you prioritize spending time with God in your daily life? What practices or habits can you develop to deepen your intimacy with God?

_____

_____

_____

Waiting on God's timing can be challenging. In what areas of your life are you waiting for God to answer prayers or fulfill your desires? While waiting, how can you actively delight in the Lord and live a life that pleases him?

_____

_____

_____

PRAYER

Dear Heavenly Father, thank you for your promise in Psalm 37:4. If I take delight in you, you will give me the desires of my heart. Lord, like David. I desire to live with you every moment, but I honestly don't know how to delight in you continually. Teach me, Lord, how to delight in your will, to walk in honesty and obedience, to come before you in prayer, and to live a righteous life according to your commands. Help me make you the genuine desire of my heart, for in seeking you, I will find all I need. I need peace, restoration, and healing in this season of waiting and expectancy. I trust in your promises, knowing that you will provide everything I need as I seek your kingdom above all else. In Jesus's name, I pray. Amen.

TRUSTING GOD'S GUIDANCE

Let me hear of your unfailing love each morning, for I am trusting you. Show me where to walk, for I give myself to you. (Psalm 143:8)

It's important to remember we are in a close relationship and partnership with God. We can trust him with our past, present, and future, knowing he will guide us through any situation and help us take the necessary steps in our journey.

He will give us the wisdom to make the right decisions and the courage to take bold steps of faith when we can't see where we're going. Like a loving parent, God wants us to know he is always there for us and will provide everything we need.

Trusting in God is like children depending on their parents. Children rely on their parents to provide for their needs and plan their future. Similarly, God wants us to trust him completely, knowing he will always provide for us because he loves us. Just like parents who prepare for and anticipate their children's needs, God knows what we need and will take care of us.

When we think about how much God loves and cares for us, we realize he knows us better than we know ourselves and wants the best for us. He created us with a unique purpose and has the answers we need to live a fulfilling life. We can trust in his guidance and take comfort in the fact he is always there for us, no matter what.

Sometimes, we hit a breaking point and feel like we've blown a fuse. But knowing God knows how to get us re-ignited is comforting. He created us with a unique purpose and has all the answers we need to live a fulfilling life. That's why it's so important to stay closely connected to him. We can access healing, peace, and the power to fulfill our God-created purpose.

I've discovered God has a bigger picture for our lives. Sometimes, the things we want may not be the best for us, and God knows better than anyone. He's always there to guide us and keep us safe, even when we may not understand the reasons behind his decisions. We find the strength to fulfill our God-given purpose as we continue to trust in him and stay connected.

It's natural to feel frustrated when things don't go according to plan. But sometimes, those delays mean we need to hold on a bit longer for God's guidance. When struggling to solve a problem, it might be time to seek the advice of a subject-matter expert who can offer valuable insights. Ultimately, we can trust that God is the ultimate expert in our lives and will guide us toward the best possible outcome.

Trying to figure out solutions on your own can be overwhelming. Trusting in God and letting him guide you through life's challenges is essential. He is like a dance partner, leading and navigating you through the twists and turns of life. If you're feeling lost or unsure, take some time to quiet your mind and listen to his small voice. Remember, God is the expert in your life and will always lead you toward the best possible outcome.

SCRIPTURES ABOUT GOD'S LEADING

ISAIAH 48:17: "This is what the LORD says—your Redeemer, the Holy One of Israel: 'I am the LORD your God, who teaches you what is good for you and leads you along the paths you should follow.'"

PSALM 16:11: "You will show me the way of life, granting me the joy of your presence and the pleasures of living with you forever."

PSALM 119:105: "Your word is a lamp to guide my feet and a light for my path."

PROMISES WHEN GOD LEADS

PROMISE OF WISDOM. PROVERBS 4:11: "I will teach you wisdom's ways and lead you in straight paths."

PROMISE OF BEING RESCUED. PSALM 34:18-19: "The LORD is close to the brokenhearted; he rescues those whose spirits are crushed. The righteous person faces many troubles, but the LORD comes to the rescue each time."

PROMISE OF OLD THINGS BECOMING NEW. 2 CORINTHIANS 5:17: "This means that anyone who belongs to Christ has become a new person. The old life is gone; a new life has begun!"

GRACE TO REBUILD

How is your relationship with God? Are there aspects of your life where trusting God feels easier, and what areas do you find challenging?

_____

_____

_____

Recall the last time you took a huge leap of faith, not knowing where it would lead. What happened afterward? What did you learn from that experience about how God guides and provides, even in uncertain times?

_____

_____

_____

What do you think about God being like a loving parent, always looking out for you? How does this perspective influence the level of trust you have in him? Are there specific areas in your life where you must relinquish control and trust God completely?

_____

_____

_____

PRAYER

Dear Heavenly Father, I trust you with my past, present, and future. Like a loving parent, you anticipate my needs and lead me through life's twists. Help me trust you completely, surrendering my fears. You know me intimately, and you have a unique purpose for my life. I rely on you for my healing, peace, and strength. You are my constant guide, leading me along the right path. In Jesus's name, I pray. Amen.

NAVIGATING GOD'S WILL THROUGH TRANSITION

"So we have not stopped praying for you since we first heard about you. We ask God to give you complete knowledge of his will and to give you spiritual wisdom and understanding. Then, the way you live will always honor and please the LORD, and your lives will produce every kind of good fruit. All the while, you will grow as you learn to know God better and better." (Colossians1:9-10)

How often have you thought "I want to be in God's will for my life?" Discovering God's will isn't easy, especially when we are unclear about our purpose. The Bible reminds us that "When people do not accept divine guidance, they run wild. But whoever obeys the law is joyful" (Proverbs 29:18). This scripture says if we don't have a vision from God, we will run wild and be scattered. If we stay in this place, we might never discover God's will (vision) for us.

The enemy wants to convince us that we are no longer qualified to serve and minister because of our marital status change. He is okay with us thinking about our vision and purpose in God, but he sure doesn't want us to start seeing, planning, and executing God's vision. Be encouraged. Our vision and purpose in God have not been canceled because of divorce or separation.

God has a beautiful plan and will use our transitions as part of his overall strategy of bringing us into his purpose for our lives. Therefore, it's essential to pursue God's will even in transition. Here are some results of being out of God's will and rewards for being in his will.

RESULTS OF STRAYING FROM GOD'S WILL:

LACK OF DISCIPLINE. PROVERBS 25:28: "A person without self-control is like a city with broken-down walls."

DESTRUCTION. PROVERBS 14:12: "There is a path before each person that seems right, but it ends in death."

UNHAPPINESS. PSALM 32:10: "Many sorrows come to the wicked, but unfailing love surrounds those who trust the LORD."

REWARDS FOR BEING IN GOD'S WILL

SATISFACTION. COLOSSIANS 3:23: "Work willingly at whatever you do, as though you were working for the Lord rather than for people."

HAPPINESS. PSALM 37:4: "Take delight in the LORD, and he will give you your heart's desires."

INCREASED DISCERNMENT. PSALM 25:9: "He leads the humble in doing right, teaching them his way."

God doesn't always clearly reveal his will all at once. Sometimes, he places breadcrumbs in our path, leading us to where we should go. At other times, he puts a desire in us to do something and the passion to pursue it until it gets done. If we want to discover God's will, we must lay aside our will, let him have the final say, and, most importantly, obey.

When we start walking according to God's will, we'll experience courage and boldness in a way we had not previously experienced. Those dark, fearful places that were once intimidating are not so scary now. Being in God's will is the safest and best place possible.

SCRIPTURES ABOUT NAVIGATING GOD'S WILL THROUGH TRANSITION

ISAIAH 30:21: "Your own ears will hear him. Right behind you, a voice will say, 'This is the way you should go,' whether to the right or to the left."

JAMES 1:5: "If you need wisdom, ask our generous God, and he will give it to you. He will not rebuke you for asking."

PSALM 37:23: "The LORD directs the steps of the godly. He delights in every detail of their lives."

PROMISES WHEN GOD NAVIGATES US
THROUGH TRANSITION

PROMISE OF GUIDANCE CONTINUALLY. PSALM 48:14: "For that is what God is like. He is our God forever and ever, and he will guide us until we die."

PROMISE OF DIRECTION. PSALM 73:24: "You guide me with your counsel, leading me to a glorious destiny."

PROMISE OF A NEW PATH. ISAIAH 42:16: "I will lead blind Israel down a new path, guiding them along an unfamiliar way. I will brighten the darkness before them and smooth out the road ahead of them. Yes, I will indeed do these things; I will not forsake them."

GRACE TO REBUILD

How often have you contemplated the desire to be in God's will for your life, especially during transition and change? What are some of the specific transitions you're currently facing or have faced in the past?

_____

_____

_____

In Proverbs 29:18, the Bible tells us that without a vision from God, people tend to run wild and become scattered. Have you ever experienced a time when you felt spiritually adrift or uncertain about your purpose and direction? How did that affect you?

_____

_____

_____

The enemy often tries to convince us we are disqualified from serving and ministering to others, primarily based on life circumstances. Have you ever felt this way? How do you combat such thoughts and stay focused on God's purpose for your life?

_____

_____

_____

PRAYER

Dear Heavenly Father, I seek your guidance during times of change and transition. I desire to be in your will because I will lose my way without your direction. Based on my circumstances, I rebuke the enemy's attempts to disqualify me from serving you and others. Instead, I trust your plan for my life. Thank you for the rewards of staying faithful to your will. Lord, guide me continually, lead me to my destiny, and illuminate my path in times of darkness. I surrender my will to yours, knowing your will is the safest and best place to be.

In Jesus's name, I pray. Amen.

PART 5

HOPE FOR A HEALED HEART

*He heals the brokenhearted and bandages
their wounds. (Psalm 147:3)*

DAY 21

THE POWER OF LETTING GO

PART 1

Why am I discouraged? Why is my heart so sad? I will put my hope in God! I will praise him again— my Savior and my God! (Psalm 42:11)

As Christian women, we are not exempt from pain. God didn't promise we wouldn't have to deal with pain. Instead, he promised to be with us as we endure our painful circumstances. As a woman in ministry, I didn't know how to deal with the emotional impact of my divorce effectively.

Facing rejection, abandonment, betrayal, disappointment, shame, and embarrassment led to significant trust challenges. These issues hindered my ability to openly communicate my emotions due to fears of being misunderstood and judgment, particularly concerning my failed marriage.

Because I had a "D" on my life's report card, I felt my only viable solution was to step away from ministry. I had failed God and the expectations of others. The divorce had taken me two giant steps backward in walking fully into my God-created purpose. How could God possibly rebuild my life? My marriage was my ministry. How could God use me now that I am damaged? Although I felt destroyed, God was doing something unique for me behind the scenes.

I became desperate to move beyond the stigma of the "D," but something was holding me back. I was severely disappointed. If I followed all the correct spiritual and relational principles, my life would automatically fall into place because I was doing everything right. But as time passed, I realized my formula for a perfect life wasn't adding up.

Despite diligently doing everything right, my life continued to unravel, presenting a perplexing contradiction that haunted me for years. I found myself consumed by the injustice of my circumstances, concluding that right actions could lead to wrong outcomes. This conflict created a deep sense of disappointment and many unanswered questions within me.

Major disappointments can be challenging to understand and move past. We can get stuck in a negative thinking pattern, making us resist letting go and embracing a different perspective or new plan God might be conjuring up. At times, our determination will have us carrying a sign that reads, "I'll never give up," even though the weight of the battle is overwhelming us.

Fighting for our marriage is commendable. However, there are occasions when God intends to alleviate us from the emotional heaviness we bear. This includes releasing preconceived notions about how God should restore us and what's best for us. Instead, we should remain receptive to his unique plan, even when it initially doesn't seem logical.

Letting go of the disappointments of my failed marriage was hard because it required me to go to a deeper level of forgiveness. I blamed my ex for the divorce. He popped my balloons for the dreams and goals I envisioned. I was sad. I thought I had forgiven him, but God showed me I was holding on to unforgiveness because of the disappointments I faced.

You may be trying to sort through some disappointments. You could be questioning why you are not seeing the return on the time, effort, and sacrifices you have invested into your relationship. It's possible you are not able to let go of your disappointing feelings. God wants you to release disappointments to his tender and loving care.

Today, he is extending his hand to remind you he can be trusted—your disappointments are safe with him. He has a beautiful plan to turn disappointments into divine appointments.

SCRIPTURES ABOUT LETTING GO

PHILIPPIANS 3:13-14: "No, dear brothers and sisters, I have not achieved it, but I focus on this one thing: Forgetting the past and looking forward to what lies ahead, I press on to reach the end of the race and receive the heavenly prize for which God, through Christ Jesus, is calling us."

EPHESIANS 4:31-32: "Get rid of all bitterness, rage, anger, harsh words, and slander, as well as all types of evil behavior. Instead, be kind to each other, tenderhearted, forgiving one another, just as God through Christ has forgiven you."

PSALM 62:8: "O my people, trust in him at all times. Pour out your heart to him, for God is our refuge."

PROMISES WHEN WE LET GO

PROMISE OF CARE. 1 PETER 5:7: "Give all your worries and cares to God, for he cares about you."

PROMISE OF STRENGTH DURING WEAKNESS. 2 CORINTHIANS 12:9: "Each time he said, 'My grace is all you need. My power works best in weakness.' So now I am glad to boast about my weaknesses so that the power of Christ can work through me."

PROMISE OF COMFORT AND GOD'S PRESENCE. PSALM 23:4: "Even when I walk through the darkest valley, I will not be afraid, for you are close beside me. Your rod and your staff protect and comfort me."

GRACE TO REBUILD

Have you been dealing with any disappointments or burdens that are hard to shake off? What emotions surface when you reflect on these challenges? Do you think any of these struggles have affected you spiritually in any way?

_____

_____

_____

Ever thought about letting go of this burden and giving it to God? Do you have specific ideas about how you want God to assist you in releasing this burden?

_____

_____

_____

Do you have any specific strategies for overcoming disappointment and placing your faith in God's plan for renewal? Are there particular actions or changes you could implement to demonstrate that you're entrusting your struggles to God's compassionate care?

_____

_____

_____

PRAYER

Dear Heavenly Father, I come to you burdened by disappointments and pain. I've struggled to let go of the past and the hurt it has brought. I confess my doubts and fears, wondering how you can rebuild my life after the loss I've experienced. I understand now your ways are not always my ways. I release my expectations and trust in your perfect plan. Help me let go of my understanding and embrace your guidance. I also recognize the need for more forgiveness.

I release any unforgiveness in my heart and forgive those who have caused me pain. I pray for others facing similar struggles. May they find the strength to release their burdens into your loving care, knowing you can be trusted. Thank you for your promises of restoration, strength, and comfort. I trust you are rebuilding my life into a testimony of your faithfulness. In Jesus's name, I pray. Amen.

THE POWER OF LETTING GO
PART 2

Hear my prayer, O LORD; listen to my plea! Answer me
because you are faithful and righteous. (Psalm 143:1)

I discovered an essential step to letting go of emotional pain. In the prior devotion, I mentioned I needed to let go of some disappointments, but I didn't know how. One day, after praying, I was inspired to write a letter of release to God. In this letter, I shared my disappointments with him, and, surprisingly, my heart responded beautifully. It started to heal.

My letter:

Dear God, I'm writing this letter as a desperate prayer to release the pain I'm processing as I walk through this divorce. I'm at a place where I don't expect or need an apology to forgive or move on. I only need to know you are with me.

I can see the good you are birthing in me through this painful place. I'm getting to a place of being thankful for it. If I hadn't taken the time to walk through my pain and not stuff it as I did in the past, I would have missed out on seeing what you have created me to be.

Today, you spoke to me about who I am and gave me a key to ease my pain and walk in new freedom. You told me I should hear your voice louder than the voice of the enemy.

Your message was eye-opening because the harmful lies the enemy has spoken over me for years have crippled me. I have allowed the enemy's voice to consume me and throw darts of insecurities, fears, disappointments, and comparisons at my heart. These darts have penetrated my heart deeply. They have convinced me I will never heal. These darts have also disqualified me and labeled me as not having a credible voice to minister and fulfill your plans and purpose for my life.

So today, I wage war on the voice of the enemy by counteracting his lies with the truth You have spoken over me in Scripture. I let go of the past. I release all emotional pain at the feet of Jesus, and I press into the resurrection and restorative power of the cross.

I know the Holy Spirit is interceding for me now. This intercession is powerful and filled with blessings and favors for my life. I need your help to change my confession to agree with the intercession and plans you have for my future.

I let go of:

The emotional prison of the years of neglect, rejection, abandonment, and lack of approval. I am set free from being negatively defined over the years. I no longer play the negative tapes in my mind—help me destroy all negative recordings.

Hiding emotional pain because I thought that was my role as a Christian woman.

The lie that says I'm not good enough. When the enemy tells me, "You can do everything 100 percent right, and it still wouldn't be good enough," I will remind him I am the apple of your eye.

The lie of perfectionism. No more thinking I must perform flawlessly to be loved or make others feel secure, respected, and needed.

The trust issues from the betrayal.

Taking responsibility to help heal others' brokenness.

Not feeling valued or loved.

Disappointment of not being chosen first.

Being seen as a human doing (someone only validated by what I do) instead of a human being (someone validated because of my intrinsic value).

God, teach me the real meaning of your love and how it is supposed to act. Based on 1 Corinthians 13 (MSG), I understand how love is not supposed to work according to your original plan:

Love never gives up.

Love cares more for others than for self.

Love doesn't want what it doesn't have.

Love doesn't strut,

Doesn't have a swelled head,

Doesn't force itself on others,

Isn't always "me first,"

Doesn't fly off the handle,

Doesn't keep score of the sins of others,

Doesn't revel when others grovel,

Takes pleasure in the flowering of truth,

Puts up with anything,

Trusts God always,

Always looks for the best,

Never looks back,

But keeps going to the end."

Thank you, God, for helping me push past this storm. If it hadn't been for you, who was on my side, where would I be? Certainly not where I am today. You taught me the gift of pain.

If I press into the pain according to your model, you will mold me into your image—a woman free to show her scars so others can heal and who only wants to lean on you to fill every void in her life.

I love our friendship, and you show me how to search for love in all the right places instead of the wrong places. I see my value now, God. There is no way I will sell out to low bidders who try to devalue my worth, including the enemy. Because of your love, I'm free today to walk as you have created me. Amen.

One of the best gifts we can give ourselves is to honor our past by forgiving others and ourselves. We don't need to figure out our healing prescription. God has a customized solution to heal us. Let's release what we can't control or understand to God and allow him to use our pain to create our beautiful redemptive story.

SCRIPTURES ABOUT HOW TO RELEASE THINGS TO GOD

1 Thessalonians 5:16-18: "Always be joyful. Never stop praying. Be thankful in all circumstances, for this is God's will for you who belong to Christ Jesus."

Matthew 6:6: "But when you pray, go away by yourself, shut the door behind you, and pray to your Father in private. Then your Father, who sees everything, will reward you."

Matthew 7:7-8: "Keep on asking, and your will receive what you ask for. Keep on seeking, and you will find. Keep on knocking, and the door will be opened to you. For everyone who asks, receives. Everyone who seeks, finds. And to everyone who knocks, the door will be opened."

PROMISES WHEN WE RELEASE THINGS TO GOD IN PRAYER

PROMISE OF POWER. JAMES 5:16: "Confess your sins to each other and pray for each other so that you may be healed. The earnest prayer of a righteous person has great power and produces wonderful results."

PROMISE OF HEARING AND RECEIVING WHAT WE ASK. 1 JOHN 5:15: "And since we know he hears us when we make our requests, we also know that he will give us what we ask for."

PROMISE OF PEACE. 1 TIMOTHY 2:1-2: "I urge you, first of all, to pray for all people. Ask God to help them; intercede on their behalf, and give thanks for them. Pray this way for kings and all who are in authority so that we can live peaceful and quiet lives marked by godliness and dignity."

GRACE TO REBUILD

Have you ever experienced the power of prayer in releasing emotional pain or burdens? Describe the situation and how prayer impacted your experience.

_____

_____

_____

Reflect on the letter of release shared in the devotion. What aspects of it, if any, resonate with your journey or feelings? Do you have something specific you need to release to God right now?

_____

_____

_____

Are there areas in your life where you've been trying to figure out your healing prescription? How can you release control and trust God's plan for your healing and restoration?

_____

_____

_____

PRAYER

Dear Heavenly Father, I release my pain and burdens to you. Thank you for the growth I can find in my struggles. You've shown me the power of hearing your voice above the enemy's lies. I renounce those lies and choose freedom in you. I let go of the past and release my pain at the foot of the cross. Holy Spirit, thank you for interceding for me. Help me align my confessions with your plans for my future. I release perfectionism, trust issues, and the need to heal others. I long to find unconditional love, freedom, and my worth in my relationship with you. I refuse to settle for less than your best. Thank you for teaching me through my pain. I trust your customized healing process and embrace the beautiful redemptive story you are working on in my life. In Jesus's name, I pray. Amen.

HEALING FROM THE SOURCE

Yet I am confident I will see the LORD's goodness while I am here in the land of the living. Wait patiently for the LORD. Be brave and courageous. Yes, wait patiently for the LORD. (Psalm 27:13-14)

One day, I had a dream. Jesus and I were on top of a mountain, and I was stooped low with a sad look on my face. He stood a few feet away, compassionately looking at me. Then Jesus extended his hand toward me and walked closer. I hesitated. Why is he extending his hand?

This mountain had many potholes. Was the mountain's rocky terrain an indicator of where my life was headed? Would Jesus give me some bad news?

My healing process wasn't complete, but I had come a long way, so I did not want to take any steps backward. With fear in my voice, I asked if I was about to go through another wilderness experience.

To my surprise, Jesus said, "No. I'm here to take you to the other side of your pain."

Hand in hand, we leaped across the mountain.

My perspective shifted after the dream. What was on the other side? Healing? Had Jesus come to heal me? Seeking healing apart from that which points us back to God during stressful times is common and understandable, but those sources don't offer sustainable recovery.

Keep trusting Jesus. Don't give up because you will get to the other side. Life holds so much to anticipate. The divorce or separation may mark the end of one chapter, but it's not the end of our life's story. We each hold the pen to write our own vibrant chapters, filled with growth, joy, and the promise of new beginnings that lie ahead in our individual journeys.

Regardless of our past or present challenging circumstances, we are not disqualified in God's eyes. He uses the broken, the abused, the divorced, and the separated to fulfill significant roles in his divine plan. Our broken relationship doesn't define us. Our heavenly identity defines us. On our healing journey, we must continue to lean into the source of all healing, Jesus Christ. He is our trustworthy foundation of healing, comfort, hope, and everything we need.

SCRIPTURES ABOUT JESUS BEING OUR HEALER

ISAIAH 53:4-5: "Yet it was our weaknesses he carried; it was our sorrows that weighed him down. And we thought his troubles were a punishment from God, a punishment for his own sins! But he was pierced for our rebellion, crushed for our sins. He was beaten so we could be whole. He was whipped so we could be healed."

MATTHEW 11:28-30: "Then Jesus said, 'Come to me, all of you who are weary and carry heavy burdens, and I will give you rest. Take my yoke upon you. Let me teach you because I am humble and gentle at heart, and you will find rest for your souls. For my yoke is easy to bear, and the burden I give you is light.'"

2 CORINTHIANS 1:3-4: "All praise to God, the Father of our Lord Jesus Christ. God is our merciful Father and the source of all comfort. He comforts us in all our troubles so that we can comfort others. When they are troubled, we will be able to give them the same comfort God has given us."

PROMISES FOR HEALING

PROMISE OF VIBRANT HEALTH. PSALM 30:2: "O LORD my God, I cried to you for help, and you restored my health."

PROMISE OF TRANSFORMED THINKING. ROMANS 12:2: "Don't copy the behavior and customs of this world, but let God transform you into a new person by changing the way you think. Then you will learn to know God's will for you, which is good and pleasing and perfect."

PROMISE OF A RENEWED MIND AND HEART. JOHN 14:27: "I am leaving you with a gift—peace of mind and heart. And the peace I give is a gift the world cannot give. So don't be troubled or afraid."

GRACE TO REBUILD

Have you experienced challenging, rocky seasons leaving you fearful or drained? Take time to journal about those moments and how you coped.

_____

_____

_____

Consider the dream described in the devotional. Imagine Jesus extending his hand to take you to the other side of your pain. How would you respond?

_____

_____

_____

What are the external sources or coping mechanisms you have relied on in the past? How have these sources pointed you to the healing only fully offered by Jesus?

_____

_____

_____

PRAYER

Dear Heavenly Father, I'm grateful for the promise of healing. While facing rocky seasons, I've sought healing from various sources, but I now understand true healing comes from you. Thank you for the vision of how Jesus can lead me to the other side of my pain. Help me trust your unwavering love and care, and never lose hope. I pray for others who are also healing from emotional pain from a broken relationship. Pour out your healing, peace, and strength on them today. In Jesus's name, I pray. Amen.

FROM BETRAYAL TO BLESSINGS

But Joseph replied, "Don't be afraid of me. Am I God, that I can punish you? You intended to harm me, but God intended it all for good. He brought me to this position so I could save the lives of many people. No, don't be afraid. I will continue to take care of you and your children." So he reassured them by speaking kindly to them. (Genesis 50:19-21)

The story of Joseph is recorded in Genesis 37:1–50:26. Joseph was one of Jacob's twelve sons. Jacob loved him more than his other children, so he made him a tunic of many colors.

Joseph was confident and self-assured, and being aware of his status as his father's favorite increased his self-esteem, but Joseph's siblings didn't like him for obvious reasons. They harbored jealousy and resentment toward him because of his confidence and their father's favoritism.

During the family tension, Joseph experienced two dreams. In each, his brothers were bowing down to him. When he shared the details of his dreams with his brothers, they hated him more. They plotted to kill him by casting him into a pit, hoping wild animals would devour him. However, his oldest brother decided not to leave him in the pit, so they sold Joseph into slavery for twenty shekels of silver, which equates to about $5.00 in US dollars today.

Joseph's brothers were consumed with anger, which can prevent us from seeing and doing what is right. Unchecked anger can lead to bitterness and, at its worst, murder. Divorce or separation can make us angry and unstable, causing our energy level and mental capacity to become off-balanced. When our thinking becomes foggy, we can become overwhelmed by stress and anxiety to the point where we can't function. Unwise decisions can be made in the heat of anger, so we must quickly identify any angry thoughts and align them with God's Word. We can rely on prayer, reading scripture, and asking the Holy Spirit to help us calm our angry thoughts.

Joseph's life took many disappointing turns caused by evil plots, false accusations, and neglect, but God was with him. Genesis 39:2-3 reminds us that the Lord was with Joseph and made all he did prosper. Here is how Joseph prospered:

1. He rose from being a prisoner to reigning as the second man in charge of Egypt.

2. He had favor with kings.

3. He was sensitive to the things of God.

4. He prepared a nation to survive a seven-year famine.

With God's help, Joseph realized he could survive anything. His story teaches us what matters most is how we respond to adverse events and circumstances. Eventually, Joseph's brothers asked him to forgive them because they feared Joseph would repay them with evil. Scripture never mentions Joseph plotting any revenge toward his brothers.

Instead, he forgives and tells them not to be afraid because what they meant for evil against him, God used for good.

How was Joseph able to forgive? He understood how much God loved him. His love for God was more significant than his hate for his brothers. Joseph's hard times made him resilient and forgiving. God had a bigger plan for him—to save lives.

SCRIPTURES ABOUT BETRAYAL

PSALM 55:12-14: "It is not an enemy who taunts me—I could bear that. It is not my foes who so arrogantly insult me—I could have hidden from them. Instead, it is you—my equal, my companion and close friend. What good fellowship we once enjoyed as we walked together to the house of God."

MATTHEW 26:48-50: "The traitor, Judas, has given them a pre-arranged signal: 'You will know which one to arrest when I greet him with a kiss.' So Judas came straight to Jesus. 'Greetings Rabbi!' he exclaimed and gave him the kiss. Jesus said, 'My friend, go ahead and do what you have come for.' Then the others grabbed Jesus and arrested him."

2 TIMOTHY 3:1-4: "You should know this, Timothy, that in the last days there will be very difficult times. For people will love only themselves and their money. They will be boastful and proud, scoffing at God, disobedient to their parents, and ungrateful. They will consider nothing sacred. They will be unloving and unforgiving; they will slander others and have no self-control. They will be cruel and hate what is good. They will betray their friends, be reckless, be puffed up with pride, and love pleasure rather than God."

PROMISES WHEN WE FACE BETRAYAL

PROMISE OF PROTECTION. PSALM 32:7: "For you are my hiding place; you protect me from trouble. You surround me with songs of victory."

PROMISE OF GOD'S HELP. PSALM 37:5: "Commit everything you do to the LORD. Trust him, and he will help you."

PROMISE OF VINDICATION. ISAIAH 54:17: "But in that coming day, no weapon turned against you will succeed. You will silence every voice raised up to accuse you. These benefits are enjoyed by the servants of the LORD; their vindication will come from me. I, the LORD, have spoken!"

GRACE TO REBUILD

Reflect on your experience with divorce or separation. How did you initially react to the situation? Did you feel betrayed, hurt, or angry? How might Joseph's ability to forgive inspire you?

_____

_____

_____

Consider Joseph's capacity to forgive his brothers despite the betrayal he endured. What do you need to begin the process of forgiveness, both for your well-being and as an expression of trust in God's plan for your future?

_____

_____

_____

Choose one of the scriptures in the "Promises When We Face Betrayal" section (for example, Psalm 32:7, Psalm 37:5, or Isaiah 54:17) and reflect on how it applies to your situation. How can knowing God offers protection, help, and vindication bring hope and healing during divorce or separation?

_____

_____

_____

PRAYER

Dear Heavenly Father, Reflecting on Joseph's story, I come before you with a heavy heart. I've felt the sting of betrayal and the weight of disappointment. Like Joseph, I've faced hurt and anger, struggling to forgive those who've deeply wounded me. Please give me the courage and grace to release these burdens to you. Help me find peace during the storm of emotions, drawing inspiration from Joseph's forgiveness. Please give me the wisdom to embrace forgiveness, see beyond the hurt, and trust in your restoration. Guide me to move forward with grace, patience, and fresh hope, believing my circumstances are improving daily. In Jesus's name, I pray. Amen.

WHAT'S IN A NAME?

Joseph named his older son Manasseh, for he said, "God has made
me forget all my troubles and everyone in my father's family."
Joseph named his second son Ephraim, for he said, "God has
made me fruitful in this land of my grief." (Genesis 41:51-52)

Parents invest considerable time and thought into choosing their children's names. They might select a name based on family tradition or preference. The name could also be chosen with the hope that it carries a significant meaning or conveys their aspirations for their child's future.

Joseph was blessed to have two sons, and he chose their names based on preference. Each name reflected his journey from adversity to prosperity and his gratitude for God's faithfulness in helping him forget past hardships and restore his life. The names of the sons of Joseph were Manasseh and Ephraim. The meanings of their names have much importance:

❧ Manasseh means making to forget or causing to forget. When Joseph named his firstborn son Manasseh, God made him forget all his toil. Joseph was grateful to God for helping him overcome his hardships and trials.

෴ Ephraim comes from the Hebrew word to be fruitful or to bear fruit. Joseph gave this name to his second son because God made him fruitful despite his afflictions.

Years ago, I discovered the meaning of my name. Tracy means war-like, fighter, or brave warrior. I had reservations about the definition because I interpreted it as having a negative connotation. I didn't want to be associated with being a fighter or engaging in conflict. However, my view of my name changed during my divorce while I encountered many conflicting forces.

Unbeknownst to my parents, they named me Tracy, the fighter, because one day I would need a warlike character to be victorious in the fight of my life—my divorce. My character had to transform into the definition of my name to survive.

Ephesians 6:12 reminds us that "For we are not fighting against flesh-and-blood enemies, but against evil rulers and authorities of the unseen world, against mighty powers in this dark world, and against evil spirits in the heavenly places."

The divorce or separation fight is spiritual. I'm not a fighter physically, but I had to learn how to fight the enemy. Ephesians 6:13-18 gives us a powerful strategy to use when fighting against the enemy:

> "Therefore, put on every piece of God's armor so you will be able to resist the enemy in the time of evil. Then after the battle, you will still be standing firm. Stand your ground, putting on the belt of truth and the body armor of God's righteousness. For shoes, put on the peace that comes from the Good News so that you will be fully prepared. In addition to all of these, hold up the shield of faith to stop the fiery arrows of the devil. Put on salvation as your helmet, and take the sword of the Spirit, which is the word of God. Pray in

the Spirit at all times and on every occasion. Stay alert and be persistent in your prayers for all believers everywhere."

Despite the challenges we face, our life experiences can reveal new qualities of our character and identity. When we confront the battles of life, we can adopt new names or qualities to reflect our resilience, growth, and ability to withstand the enemy's attacks. Our names can remind us of our courage and the blessings awaiting us on the other side of adversity.

Joseph had to forget the sorrows he faced at his father's house before he could receive and appreciate the fruit and blessings from God. It is possible to forget the negative memories leading up to and during your separation or divorce. However, forgetting our past requires us to trust God and continue asking him how to give him glory in our battles.

SCRIPTURES ABOUT GOD'S NAMES FOR HIS DAUGHTERS

PSALM 139:14: "Thank you for making me so wonderfully complex! Your workmanship is marvelous—how well I know it."

COLOSSIANS 3:12: "Since God chose you to be the holy people he loves, you must clothe yourselves with tenderhearted mercy, kindness, humility, gentleness, and patience."

1 PETER 2:9: "But you are not like that, for you are a chosen people. You are royal priests, a holy nation, God's very own possession. As a result, you can show others the goodness of God, for he called you out of the darkness into his wonderful light."

PROMISES OF BEING GOD'S DAUGHTERS

PROMISE OF BEING BELOVED. EPHESIANS 5:1: "Imitate God, therefore, in everything you do, because you are his dear children."

PROMISE OF FORGIVENESS AND REDEMPTION. EPHESIANS 1:7: "He is so rich in kindness and grace that he purchased our freedom with the blood of his Son and forgave our sins."

PROMISE OF BEING CO-HEIRS WITH CHRIST. ROMANS 8:17: "And since we are his children, we are his heirs. In fact, together with Christ we are heirs of God's glory. But if we are to share his glory, we must also share his suffering."

GRACE TO REBUILD

Reflect on the significance of your name. What does your name mean, and how do you feel about its meaning? Have you considered how your name might relate to your life experiences and challenges? Write about any connections or thoughts you have regarding your name.

_____

_____

_____

Consider the story of Joseph and his sons' names—Manesseh and Ephraim. Think about the names you might choose for yourself based on your life journey and experiences. If you were to adopt a new name or quality to reflect your resilience and growth, what would it be? And why?

_____

_____

_____

How have you experienced spiritual battles during your divorce or separation? Reflect on the pieces of God's armor (truth, righteousness, peace, faith, salvation, the Word of God, and prayer) and how they have been relevant in your journey. Write about your strategies for standing firm against spiritual challenges.

_____

_____

_____

PRAYER

Dear Heavenly Father, I'm grateful for the name(s) you have given me. I thank you for the lessons learned from the story of Joseph. As I face life's battles, please grant me the strength to wear the full armor to stand firm against the enemy's attacks. Lord, help me choose new names and qualities that align with your purpose for me, reminding me of the courage and blessings awaiting me after adversity. I desire to glorify you in my battles and follow your plan. In Jesus's name, I pray. Amen.

PART 6

HOPE TO DREAM AGAIN

For everything there is a season, a time for every activity under heaven.
A time to kill and a time to heal.
A time to tear down and a time to build up.
A time to cry and a time to laugh.
A time to grieve and a time to dance.
A time to scatter stones and a time to gather stones.
A time to embrace and a time to turn away.
A time to search and a time to quit searching.
A time to keep and a time to throw away.
A time to tear and a time to mend.
A time to be quiet and a time to speak. (Ecclesiastes 3:1, 3-7)

A COVENANT
TO REBUILD

And now, O LORD God, I am your servant; do as you have promised concerning me and my family. May it be a promise that will last forever. And may your name be honored forever so that everyone will say, 'The LORD of Heaven's Armies is God over Israel!' And may the house of your servant David continue before you forever. (2 Samuel 7:25-26)

David was a great king, one of the best for his people, and one of God's favorites. God referred to him as a "man after his own heart." David petitioned God until he got answers, wisdom, and his approval. He sought after God, and God wanted to bless him in a huge way.

This divine blessing became evident when David moved into a grand house made of wood. In this safe and peaceful haven, he found himself shielded from his enemies, symbolizing the blessing and protection God had bestowed upon him.

Second Samuel 7:1-29 (MSG) highlights a conversation between David and Nathan:

David: "Look at this: Here I am, comfortable in a luxurious house of cedar, and the presence of God sits in a plain tent." David was troubled because his new house was more luxurious than the tent where God's presence resided. David decided he wanted to build a house for God's presence.

Nathan: "Whatever is on your heart, go and do it because God is with you!" Nathan understood God would bless whatever David put his hands and mind to do because God was always in David's heart. Nathan received a word from God about David's desire to build him a house.

This is the message God gave Nathan to convey to David:

"So here is what you are to tell my servant David: The God-of-the-Angel-Armies has this word for you: I took you from the pasture, tagging along after sheep, and made you prince over my people Israel.

I was with you everywhere you went and mowed your enemies down before you. Now I'm making you famous, to be ranked with the great names on earth.

And I'm going to set aside a place for my people, Israel, and plant them there, so they'll have their own home and not be knocked around anymore. Nor will evil men afflict you as they always have, even during the days I set judges over my people Israel. Finally, I'm going to give you peace from all your enemies.

When your life is complete and you're buried with your ancestors, then I'll raise up your child, your own flesh and blood, to succeed you, and I'll firmly establish his rule.

He will build a house to honor me, and I will guarantee his kingdom's rule permanently.

I'll be a father to him, and he'll be a son to me. When he does wrong, I'll discipline him in the usual ways, the pitfalls and obstacles of this mortal life.

But I'll never remove my gracious love from him, as I removed it from Saul, who preceded you and whom I most certainly did remove.

Your family and your kingdom are permanently secured. I'm keeping my eye on them! And your royal throne will always be there, rock solid."

Nathan conveyed to David all the details of the vision he had received from God. The covenant God gave David deeply touched him. Verses 18-29 highlight David's reaction to God's promises. This is a summary of David's response:

HUMILITY AND AMAZEMENT. David begins by expressing humility and awe at the incredible favor God showed him and his family. He acknowledges his unworthiness and recognizes God elevated him to a remarkable position in life.

GRATITUDE FOR HIS FUTURE LEGACY. David is grateful for his blessings and the glimpse into God's future regarding his family. He is overwhelmed by God's generosity.

PRAISE FOR GOD'S GREATNESS AND CHARACTER. David praises God for his greatness. He acknowledges there is no God like the LORD, and he marvels at the extraordinary acts God performed, especially in delivering the nation of Israel from Egypt.

Prayer for Blessing. David concludes by requesting God's continuous blessings on his family. He asks God to protect his family always, which God already promised, and he prays for God's blessing to be upon his family permanently.

Are you desperate to rebuild your life? Possibly, you desire vindication because someone has tarnished your name. David's story is a testament to the benefits of seeking God consistently in the face of adversity. When we stay focused on God's business, he will handle our business in a way that exceeds our expectations.

Let's ramp up our devotion to God by considering ways to honor God and magnify his name. We can also request from God a covenant to reconstruct our lives, restore our reputation, and ensure a natural and spiritual legacy for our families.

SCRIPTURES ABOUT GOD'S REBUILDING PLAN

Lamentations 3:22-23: "The faithful love of the LORD never ends! His mercies never cease. Great is his faithfulness; his mercies begin afresh each morning."

Proverbs 22:1: "Choose a good reputation over great riches; being held in high esteem is better than silver or gold."

Proverbs 3:3-4: "Never let loyalty and kindness leave you! Tie them around your neck as a reminder. Write them deep within your heart. Then you will find favor with both God and people, and you will earn a good reputation."

PROMISES TO REBUILD

PROMISE OF HONOR. 1 PETER 5:6: "So humble yourselves under the mighty power of God, and at the right time he will lift you up in honor."

PROMISE OF A DOUBLE BLESSING. JOB 42:10: "When Job prayed for his friends, the LORD restored his fortunes. In fact, the LORD gave him twice as much as before!"

PROMISE OF NO MORE DISGRACE. ISAIAH 54:4: "Fear not; you will no longer live in shame. Don't be afraid; there is no more disgrace for you. You will no longer remember the shame of your youth and the sorrows of widowhood."

GRACE TO REBUILD

Reflect on David's relentless pursuit of God. How can you intensify your pursuit of God? How can you seek him with a similar dedication and passion?

_____

_____

_____

In David's story, he desired to build a house for the presence of God. What symbolic "house" or area of your life needs rebuilding or renewal? Is it your reputation, relationships, or some other aspect? How might seeking God's guidance and covenant impact this area?

_____

_____

_____

Consider God's promises to David, including the assurance of a legacy and a secure throne. How does God's willingness to bless David and establish his family's future resonate with your desires for your life and family? What specific blessings or legacies are you seeking from God?

_____

_____

_____

PRAYER

Dear Heavenly Father, help me pursue you with unwavering dedication and passion as King David did. I have many areas needing your touch for rebuilding and renewal. Thank you for your faithfulness and promises to honor me, restore me, and provide a legacy for my family. In Jesus's name, I pray. Amen.

DO YOU BELIEVE
IN MIRACLES?

*Now all glory to God, who is able, through his mighty
power at work within us, to accomplish infinitely more
than we might ask or think. (Ephesians 3:20)*

A miracle is a personal and awe-inspiring event that defies explanation, showing us that something greater than ourselves is at work in our lives. You will know you need a miracle when you have tried everything in your strength and have consistently failed.

In Acts 3:1-10 we read a story of a crippled man since birth. His daily routine was to lay outside the temple at the "Beautiful Gate" and beg for money. One day, his life took a remarkable turn, and not because of a generous donation. Instead, he encountered two individuals who radically changed his life.

Peter and John were on their way to a prayer service at the temple. When they drew near, the disabled man requested financial assistance. Peter responded to the man's plea, stating that while he lacked silver and gold, he could offer something else: his belief in the power of Jesus Christ's name. Through this faith, Peter healed the man and told him to rise and walk, and he did.

The disabled man thought his inability to walk was a life sentence, but God had a beautiful surprise waiting for him. What if the crippled man told Peter, "I don't want what you have in the name of Jesus Christ," he would have missed out on his miracle.

We might miss out on miracles in store for us if we're not open to receiving them in unexpected ways. Sometimes, these miracles don't come as we envisioned.

Positioning ourselves to embrace a miracle mindset involves maintaining faith in the Bible as our ultimate authority during our challenges and adverse circumstances. This mindset means believing wholeheartedly in what God tells us, regardless of whether we've seen it with our own eyes.

Second Corinthians 4:18 reminds us, "So we don't look at the troubles we can see now; rather, we fix our gaze on things that cannot be seen. For the things we see now will soon be gone, but the things we cannot see will last forever." We should focus on things not seen because the troubles we endure now are temporary, while the unseen promises of God are everlasting. Our perspective should be fixed on God's promises to us, and we must remain open to his miraculous work, although it may defy our expectations. This mindset is crucial when we are facing difficult circumstances.

Perhaps you've faced challenging circumstances for a long time, leaving you hopeless about the possibility of a miracle occurring in your life. Be encouraged. God has the power to transform your situation suddenly. Don't be surprised when miracles happen.

Instead, look for them, and keep your eyes open for ways God might want to use you, like he used Peter, to be a miracle for someone else. God wants his supernatural power to become natural.

SCRIPTURES ABOUT GOD'S ABUNDANCE

PSALM 23:5: "You prepare a feast for me in the presence of my enemies. You honor me by anointing my head with oil. My cup overflows with blessings."

JOHN 10:10: "The thief's purpose is to steal and kill and destroy. My purpose is to give them a rich and satisfying life."

MALACHI 3:10: "Bring all the tithes into the storehouse so there will be enough food in my Temple. If you do," says the LORD of Heaven's Armies, "I will open the windows of heaven for you. I will pour out a blessing so great you won't have enough room to take it in! Try it! Put me to the test!"

PROMISES TO RECEIVE MORE

PROMISE OF GENEROUS PROVISIONS. 2 CORINTHIANS 9:8: "And God will generously provide all you need. Then you will always have everything you need and plenty left over to share with others."

PROMISE OF GIVING AND RECEIVING. LUKE 6:38: "Give, and you will receive. Your gift will return to you in full—pressed down, shaken together to make room for more, running over, and poured into your lap. The amount you give will determine the amount you get back."

PROMISE OF AN OVERFLOW. PROVERBS 3:9-10: "Honor the LORD with your wealth and with the best part of everything you produce. Then he will fill your barns with grain, and your vats will overflow with good wine."

GRACE TO REBUILD

Have you ever experienced a miracle in your life, big or small? Did it happen in a way you expected? Or was it unexpected?

_____

_____

_____

Reflect on your thoughts about expecting miracles. Do you find believing in things you cannot see challenging? How can you work on strengthening your faith and embracing a "miracle mindset"?

_____

_____

_____

Consider the scriptures about God's generous provisions and the other promises. Which of these promises resonate with you the most? How can you apply them all to your life to experience God's abundance and blessings more deeply?

_____

_____

_____

PRAYER

Dear Heavenly Father, thank you for the miracles you've performed in my life, both those I have seen and those I haven't yet. Your miracles come in unexpected ways beyond what I can imagine. I pray for the gift of a miracle mindset. I desire an attitude anticipating your supernatural intervention in my life and the lives of those I encounter. Increase my faith and help me trust your divine plan. I desire to trust in your promises, regardless of the challenges surrounding me. Thank you for being a God who blesses your children more than they could ever ask or imagine. In Jesus's name, I pray. Amen.

OBSTACLES: OUR NEXT BIG OPPORTUNITY

Then he said to me, "This is what the LORD says to Zerubbabel: It is not by force nor by strength, but by my Spirit, says the LORD of Heaven's Armies. Nothing, not even a mighty mountain, will stand in Zerubbabel's way; it will become a level plain before him! And when Zerubbabel sets the final stone of the temple in place, the people will shout: 'May God bless it! May God bless it!'" (Zechariah 4:6-7)

Imagine facing a wall between you and your dreams or encountering a problem blocking your path toward a goal. Obstacles can either distract us or strengthen us spiritually. They can either defeat us or elevate us to the next level. We must stay alert and recognize these obstacles as they arise, as they can hinder us from accomplishing our God-given assignments.

Consider these real-life scenarios where obstacles emerge: You may have experienced a situation where you had a great idea but found it challenging to follow through with its execution. Initially, you were excited, feeling on top of the world. However, an unexpected obstacle mysteriously appeared—a health issue, a setback in your finances, a problem with a child's teacher, or a separation or divorce.

These obstacles can slow our progress and bring our ideas to a standstill. Their ability to surprise us and evoke fear is a common struggle we all face.

This concept of facing and overcoming obstacles is illustrated powerfully in the books of Ezra, Haggai, and Zechariah, which recount the story of Zerubbabel. Appointed as the leader of the Jews and commissioned by God to rebuild the temple, Zerubbabel encountered a significant challenge: overcoming the skepticism and opposition of naysayers—Babylonians against him and the temple rebuild project. They were jealous of the Jewish people's power, zeal, worship, and determination.

Despite the opposition, Zerubbabel and the Jews started work on the temple. They trusted God, remained faithful, and obeyed God's commands until the opposition and adversity increased. Like us, Zerubbabel and the Jews become exhausted from dealing with difficult people. They stopped the temple rebuild because they got discouraged. The temple stayed half-completed for more than sixteen years.

Although God commissioned Zerubbabel to lead the temple project, fear stopped him from fulfilling what God destined him to do, but God was still faithful to Zerubbabel and the Jews. He sent the prophet Zechariah to encourage them to return to obedience and complete the temple. God told Zerubbabel his own hands would not remove the mountains (obstacles) in his life, but God's Spirit would do it for him. What a relief. The only thing Zerubbabel needed to do was obey God completely by finishing the temple project.

We can learn from Zerubbabel's example. We have a helper and an encourager—the Holy Spirit. We don't have to rely solely on our strength to overcome challenges, including the opposition and discouragement often accompanying difficult situations like divorce or separation. The Holy Spirit is here to assist us in removing obstacles from our path.

Actively cooperating with the Holy Spirit to move the mountains in our lives begins with seeking the Holy Spirit's assistance through prayer. By doing so, we invite him to encourage and collaborate with us as we navigate rebuilding our lives. Surprisingly, when we release the heavy lifting to the Holy Spirit, our obstacles can transform into significant opportunities for growth and transformation.

God is a God of multiple chances. Even when we deviate from God's original plans, encounter opposition, or become discouraged, God still has a restoration plan for us. This plan is designed to rebuild our lives, making us better than before life's circumstances attempted to tear down everything we had previously built.

SCRIPTURES ABOUT OBSTACLES BECOMING OPPORTUNITIES

ROMANS 5:3-4: "We can rejoice, too, when we run into problems and trials, for we know that they help us develop endurance. And endurance develops strength of character, and character strengthens our confident hope of salvation."

JAMES 1:2: "Dear brothers and sisters, when troubles of any kind come your way, consider it an opportunity for great joy."

2 CORINTHIANS 12:9-10: "Each time he said, 'My grace is all you need. My power works best in weakness.' So now I am glad to boast about my weaknesses so that the power of Christ can work through me. That's why I take pleasure in my weaknesses and in the insults, hardships, persecutions, and troubles that I suffer for Christ. For when I am weak, then I am strong."

PROMISES ON HOW GOD USES OUR OBSTACLES

PROMISE TO DEVELOP OUR CHARACTER. JAMES 1:3-4: "For you know that when your faith is tested, your endurance has a chance to grow. So let it grow, for when your endurance is fully developed, you will be perfect and complete, needing nothing."

PROMISE TO STRENGTHEN OUR FAITH. HEBREWS 11:6: "And it is impossible to please God without faith. Anyone who wants to come to him must believe that God exists and that he rewards those who sincerely seek him."

PROMISE TO COMFORT US SO WE CAN COMFORT OTHERS. 2 CORINTHIANS 1:3-4: "All praise to God, the Father of our Lord Jesus Christ. God is our merciful Father and the source of all comfort. He comforts us in all our troubles so that we can comfort others. When they are troubled, we will be able to give them the same comfort God has given us."

GRACE TO REBUILD

Reflect on a recent obstacle or challenge related to your separation or divorce. How did you initially react? Did you perceive the situation as a setback or an opportunity for growth?

_____

_____

_____

Zerubbabel faced significant opposition and discouragement in his mission to rebuild the temple. What kind of opposition or discouragement have you encountered while pursuing a goal or assignment? How did you handle it, and what did you learn from the experience?

_____

_____

_____

Consider the role of the Holy Spirit in your life. In what ways have you sought the Holy Spirit's guidance and assistance when facing obstacles or challenges? How can you actively cooperate with the Holy Spirit to turn obstacles into opportunities for growth and transformation?

_____

_____

_____

PRAYER

Dear Heavenly Father, I'm grateful for the lesson from Zerubbabel's story, where obstacles become opportunities. I desire to seek the Holy Spirit's guidance and strength when I face challenges and opposition. I don't want to rely solely on my abilities. Thank you for being a God of second chances and for having a restoration plan for me. Please help me embrace your plan with an open heart, trusting you are working to rebuild me better than before. I am grateful for your promises and the assurance you will use every obstacle for my good. In Jesus's name, I pray. Amen.

CHASING JOY

Always be full of joy in the Lord. I say it again—rejoice! Let everyone see that you are considerate in all you do. Remember, the Lord is coming soon. Don't worry about anything; instead, pray about everything. Tell God what you need and thank him for all he has done. Then you will experience God's peace, which exceeds anything we can understand. His peace will guard your hearts and minds as you live in Christ Jesus. (Philippians 4:4-7)

Everyone searches for happiness. The problem with happiness is that it depends on our happenings. When we go through the heartache of a loved one leaving, custody battles for children, or financial hardships, happiness goes out the window, and despair comes knocking on our door.

By contrast, joy is a deep, serene, contented place in our souls. We feel joy when we are satisfied with God's direction and purpose. Joy is supernatural because it is a gift from God. We can't fake joy because it acts as a mirror reflecting our internal state. We can pretend everything is great, but our facial expressions say otherwise. Our hearts will inform us how we score on the joy scale.

Separation and divorce can overwhelm us with disappointment, discouragement, and despair. These emotional responses are joy-robbers. We can find ourselves in a never-ending cycle of chasing after external desires to relieve our internal sadness. However, what we need most when things get crazy and rocky is a sure foundation of sustainable hope and stability, which only comes through our relationship with Jesus Christ.

Paul encourages us in Philippians 4:4 to "always be full of joy in the Lord." He is so adamant about lifting us that he repeats his sentiment. "I say it again—rejoice!" He commands us to have joy two times. Paul had experienced the highs and lows of being a Christian, and while he was in prison, he had learned through whatever he faced that having joy in the Lord encouraged and strengthened him. So now, in his letter to the church of Philippi, he thanked them for the joy they brought him and reminded them of the source of absolute joy.

In verses 4-7, Paul reminds us that joy comes when we are considerate of others, reflect on the fact Jesus is returning soon, and spend more time praying instead of worrying. When I give up my self-interest and focus on serving others, I experience joy. Also, when I think about what Jesus has done for me—he's been faithful, loving, helpful, and has assured me of his soon return—the trivialities of my current difficulties seem to fade into the background.

James 1:2 tells us to count it all joy when we go through various trails. To count means to accept or consider. We are not rejoicing because of our difficulties. Instead, we express joy because God is still good during the challenges. Let's stop keeping a record of our problems. Instead, we can ask the Lord to replace our sadness with an abundance of joy, and we can start keeping track of all the joy chasing us down.

SCRIPTURES ABOUT JOY DURING DIFFICULTIES

ROMANS 5:3-4: "We can rejoice, too, when we run into problems and trials, for we know that they help us develop endurance. And endurance develops strength of character, and character strengthens our confident hope of salvation."

JAMES 1:2-3: "Dear brothers and sisters, when troubles come your way, consider it an opportunity for great joy. For you know that when your faith is tested, your endurance has a chance to grow."

1 THESSALONIANS 5:16-18: "Always be joyful. Never stop praying. Be thankful in all circumstances, for this is God's will for you who belong to Christ Jesus."

PROMISES WHEN WE CHASE JOY

PROMISE OF HOPE. ROMANS 15:13: "I pray that God, the source of hope, will fill you completely with joy and peace because you trust in him. Then you will overflow with confident hope through the power of the Holy Spirit."

PROMISE OF FRUIT FROM THE HOLY SPIRIT. GALATIANS 5:22–23: "But the Holy Spirit produces this kind of fruit in our lives: love, joy, peace, patience, kindness, goodness, faithfulness, gentleness, and self-control. There is no law against these things!"

PROMISE OF SMILING. PROVERBS 15:13: "A glad heart makes a happy face; a broken heart crushes the spirit."

GRACE TO REBUILD

Reflect on a recent challenging situation or trial you've faced. How did your pursuit of happiness differ from seeking joy? What were the outcomes and your emotional responses in each case?

_____

_____

_____

Paul encourages us to ""always be full of joy in the Lord." How do you interpret the idea of always having joy? Is it achievable? What practical steps can you take to maintain joy, even under challenging circumstances?

_____

_____

_____

Consider the benefits of having joy during difficulties, as outlined in Romans 5:3–4, James 1:2–3, and 1 Thessalonians 5:16–18. Have you experienced personal growth and increased power through trials? How has joy played a role?

_____

_____

_____

PRAYER

Dear Heavenly Father, thank you for the reminder that true joy comes from you, even in life's challenges. Help me distinguish between fleeting happiness and enduring joy, seeking the joy in your presence. Grant me the strength to stand firm in the hope and stability of my relationship with Jesus during times of despair. Teach me to always be full of joy in you, serving others, and remembering your faithfulness and the promise of your return. May my joy be rooted in my connection with you, not external circumstances. Please guide me in recognizing and pursuing the good things you produce in me. In Jesus's name, I pray. Amen.

A NEW DAY

"So we have stopped evaluating others from a human point of view. At one time we thought of Christ merely from a human point of view. How differently we know him now! This means that anyone who belongs to Christ has become a new person. The old life is gone; a new life has begun!" (2 Corinthians 5:16-17)

At the time of writing this book, it's been almost a year since I was blessed with a new husband and a new life. We live in a lovely coastal town near San Francisco, California. We enjoy walking along a trail that runs alongside the Pacific Ocean.

We were walking our usual path one day when we began chatting about the expanse of the ocean and what lay beneath it. We considered the fish and other objects such as trash, ruins, dead animals, and even hazardous substances. The Pacific Ocean's depth ranges from 14,000–36,000 feet. If you drop something in this water, it may never be found again.

In an unexpected moment, the Lord shifted my attention to the surrounding beauty instead of the mysteries hidden beneath. The glistening water, the sound of the waves, and the majestic scenery captivated my attention. I smiled when I realized this was the answer to a prayer. I had been asking God what he wanted me to write about in the book's closing devotion. His answer was clear—he wanted me to remind you of his marvelous reconstruction plan—your new day is coming.

Sometimes, it's hard to shift our perspective to recognize the possibility of new, refreshing, and beautiful days ahead, particularly when the trash, toxicity, and wreckage of our separation or divorce are overwhelming us. What if God desires us to throw some things into the sea of forgetfulness, and in exchange, he will free us from the memories of the challenging experiences we've endured?

In Micah 7:18-19, the prophet gave a lovely prayer to God, praising him for forgetting and forgiving God's people's transgressions in the past by throwing them into the ocean:

> "Where is another God like you,
> who pardons the guilt of the remnant,
> overlooking the sins of his special people?
> You will not stay angry with your people forever,
> because you delight in showing unfailing love.
> Once again you will have compassion on us.
> You will trample our sins under your feet
> and throw them into the depths of the ocean!"

I often wondered when God would intervene supernaturally to save me from the depths of divorce. He saved me when I no longer desired to remain stuck in my pit and when I decided to partner with him and follow his path. Since God had thrown my past into the sea, I decided to do the same. I no longer desired to wear the badge of victimization that reads "pain," reminding me daily of what happened in my past.

I've forgotten those hard days because I'm no longer looking at what was behind or beneath me. I'm focused on what's ahead. Now, I can see the good in my divorce story. More than nine years ago, I would have never imagined the restoration plan God had in store for me.

People often tell me I went through my divorce with such grace. I laugh and think they have no idea the path God led me on to experience emotional healing and to release disappointments, unforgiveness, fear, and much more. I'm grateful that during my most challenging season of pain, my graceful response gave women on a similar journey hope.

God loves to restore. It's his character. I encourage you to hold onto the promises of God for hope and soul care and believe God will rebuild your life. He will supply you with a stronger spiritual foundation because you are trusting him for complete restoration for you and your family.

Take a faith step and trust God, no matter the twists and turns happening. Trust that you hear God's voice, and the Holy Spirit is leading you on the right path. God is a good Father who loves you and is invested 100 percent in your bright future. Move forward, one step at a time, holding Jesus's hand, and you will reach the other side, transitioning from your pain to your new and best life.

SCRIPTURES ABOUT A NEW DAY

PSALM 118:24: "This is the day the LORD has made. We will rejoice and be glad in it."

PSALM 30:5: "For his anger lasts only a moment, but his favor lasts a lifetime! Weeping may last through the night, but joy comes with the morning."

ISAIAH 60:1: "Arise, Jerusalem! Let your light shine for all to see. For the glory of the LORD rises to shine on you."

PROMISES FOR A NEW DAY

PROMISE OF GOD'S PROMISE BECOMING TRUE. ISAIAH 42:9: "Everything I prophesied has come true, and now I will prophesy again. I will tell you the future before it happens."

PROMISE OF THE OLD BEING FORGOTTEN. ISAIAH 65:17: "Look! I am creating a new heavens and a new earth, and no one will even think about the old ones anymore."

PROMISE OF ALL THINGS NEW. REVELATION 21:1-4: "Then I saw a new heaven and a new earth, for the old heaven and the old earth had disappeared. And the sea was also gone. And I saw the holy city, the new Jerusalem, coming down from God out of heaven like a bride beautifully dressed for her husband. I heard a loud shout from the throne, saying, 'Look, God's home is now among his people! He will live with them, and they will be his people. God himself will be with them. He will wipe every tear from their eyes, and there will be no more death or sorrow or crying or pain. All these things are gone forever."

GRACE TO REBUILD

Reflect on when you faced a significant change or a new beginning. How did you initially perceive the challenges and opportunities of this new season?

_____

_____

_____

Consider throwing past hurts, disappointments, and sins into the "ocean of forgetfulness," as described in Micah 7:18-19. What burdens or negative emotions from your past could you let go of to embrace the beauty and potential of your new day? How might this act of releasing the past impact your life?

_____

_____

_____

Reflecting on your separation or divorce. How can you take a faith step and trust God throughout the process, even when facing uncertainty? What steps can you take to move forward and embrace your new day and your best life?

_____

_____

_____

PRAYER

Dear Heavenly Father, I come before you with a heart full of gratitude for the new day. Thank you for the blessings and new beginnings you've given me. I anticipate the beauty and potential ahead, even in the face of past hurts and challenges. Lord, please help me shift my perspective. Give me the strength to let go of the burdens, disappointments, and sins of the past, just as you have cast my sins into the depths of the ocean. I believe in your promises of restoration, hope, and trust in your guidance for my future. I pray for the courage to take each step with faith, holding your hand as I journey toward the new day and my best life. May your grace empower me to rebuild and find joy in the beauty of each moment. In Jesus's name, I pray. Amen.

ACKNOWLEDGMENTS

First and foremost, my deepest thanks go to my Heavenly Father for the strength and guidance he provided while I completed this devotional. I never imagined that journaling through the most challenging seasons of my life would evolve into a book meant to uplift others facing similar trials.

A special thank you to my husband, Joe, for your unwavering support. I embarked on this book project just after our wedding, and your patience was a blessing while I dedicated many hours to writing.

I am deeply appreciative of my coach and agent, Sharon Elliott, for your keen insight and wise guidance. Your teaching and encouragement have enhanced my writing skills and helped me grow as a writer.

A heartfelt thank you to Karen and George Porter and the entire Bold Vision team. Your faith in my work and dedication to publishing materials that empower women to heal and grow spiritually were crucial in making this book a reality. I also want to express my gratitude to Larry J. Leech II for your expert editing, which tremendously streamlined the process.

To my family and many friends who have encouraged me and endorsed the book, thank you. A special thanks to my friend Amber Weigand- Buckley for your exquisite cover design and for believing in me and this project.

Finally, to everyone reading this book, thank you for allowing me to be a part of your healing journey. It's my hope that this book inspires you and reminds you of God's promises—to rebuild and beautifully restore your life!

Are you seeking support in your divorce or separation journey? The All Things New community will provide the encouragement and resources you need to heal and grow. Scan the QR code or visit the link to learn more.

https://bit.ly/allthingsnewtracyglass

MEET TRACY GLASS

TRACY GLASS, an award-winning author, speaker, and certified professional coach, is the heart of All Things New, a ministry dedicated to supporting individuals through the tough times of separation and divorce.

Her own journey inspired her to reach out, write, and create spaces for healing and learning, including a virtual coaching program and teaching Bible College classes. Tracy is deeply committed to mentoring women and helping them find strength and renewal in their faith.

In 2023, Tracy's story took a joyful turn when she married Joe, and together, they now enjoy the beauty of the San Francisco Bay Area, living proof of God's promises for new beginnings and love restored.

If you seek support and guidance through divorce or separation, reach out to Tracy at info@tracyglasscoaching.com. She is here to help you navigate this challenging time with compassion and understanding.

www.ingramcontent.com/pod-product-compliance
Lightning Source LLC
Chambersburg PA
CBHW061741120626
46550CB00005B/1849